Like Any Great Artist
Our Winning Designer Works In Oils.

Congratulations to Lars Svensson, whose winning design was chosen from over 6,000 entries in this year's "Paint The King's Car Contest." Lars' design will debut at the Daytona 500 and will appear throughout the racing season. STP and Richard would like to thank everyone from all 50 states and 9 foreign countries who created a design for the King's #43 Pontiac. In fact, picking a winner was almost as tough as winning at Daytona. And Richard should know.

SUCCESS.

The Ford Mustang Cobra of Tommy Kendall

The Ford Thunderbird of Dale Jarrett

The Ford F-150 of Scott Taylor

There were the finish lines we flew over. The winner's circles we stood proudly in. And the trophies we held high. How did we follow that success? By taking what we learned out on the hairpin turns, the pedal-to-the-metal straightaways and the

www.ford.com

SUCCESSION.

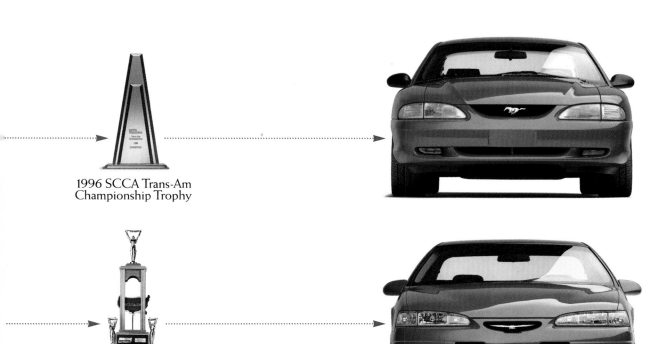

1996 SCCA Trans-Am
Championship Trophy

1996 Daytona 500
Championship Trophy*

1996 SODA Class 8
Championship Trophy

scorching desert terrain all the way to the Ford cars and trucks you can drive.
Think about it: Weekend after weekend of winning motorsports technology that has
real-world applications for the street. That's what we call taking success even farther.

WE RACE. YOU WIN.

Now it's our turn.

© 1997 B&W T Co.

Box 100's, 16 mg. "tar", 1.2 mg. nicotine av. per cigarette by FTC method.

SURGEON GENERAL'S WARNING: Quitting Smoking Now Greatly Reduces Serious Risks to Your Health.

Contents

Headliners of 1996

CART/PPG Cup

Indy Racing League

NASCAR/Winston Cup

Trans-Am Tour

IMSA Exxon WSC and GTS

Published by: Autosport International, Inc.
Publisher: John H. Norwood
Associate Publisher: Barbara Hassler-Steig
Design Director: Robert Steig
Editor: Jonathan Hughes
Front Cover Photography: Michael C. Brown, Geoffrey Hewitt, Nigel Kinrade, Steve Mohlenkamp
Contributing Photographers: Cheryl Day Anderson, Dan Bianchi, Michael C. Brown, Gary Gold, Geoffrey Hewitt, Nigel Kinrade, Walt Kuhn/IMS, Steve Mohlenkamp, Ron McQueeney/IMS, Shelly Schmidt, Bob Steig, Bob Straus, Steve Swope, Paul Webb

Motorsports America, The Men & Machines of American Motorsport, 1996-97
is published by Autosport International, Inc.
37 East 28 Street, Suite 408, New York, NY 10016
© 1997 Autosport International, Inc.
No part may be reproduced without prior written permission.
Distributed in the U.S. by Motorbooks International, Osceola, WI 54020
Printed in the U.S.A.

"Nothing reveals more about a race car and its driver than a 24-hour road race." *Hurley Haywood*

Few race car drivers have stood up to the demands of endurance racing as well as Hurley Haywood. With five wins at the *Rolex 24 at Daytona*, three at Le Mans and two at Sebring, he is the world's leading long-distance driver.

Haywood's success is a testament to his patience and discipline as much as to his skill. "In endurance racing," says Hurley, "you're always trying to stay just within the outer limits of your car. Push it too hard, and you'll never finish. Don't push

it hard enough, and you'll never win."

Staying within that zone requires remarkable precision. "A top driver consistently clocks laps within a few tenths of a second," he says. It also requires a rare empathy with the nature and quality of mechanical objects. Hurley Haywood has driven many cars to victory lane, but he has always relied on one special piece of equipment. "I've worn a Rolex for over twenty years," he says, "and it's never let me down."

ROLEX

Rolex Oyster Perpetual Daytona Cosmograph in stainless steel and 18kt gold with matching Oysterlock bracelet.
Write for brochure. Rolex Watch U.S.A., Inc., Dept. 438, Rolex Building, 665 Fifth Avenue, New York, N.Y. 10022-5383.
Rolex, ♛, Oyster Perpetual, Daytona and Oysterlock are trademarks.

SEE CLEARLY...

Since inventing the basic technology, Unelko Corporation has single-handedly pioneered the treatment of automotive glass for improved visibility and driving safety. The tried and proven RAIN-X® products can make the difference between seeing and not seeing the road, other cars and pedestrians.

NEW

Handy Wipes & Pour Pouches

NEW

Wiper Refills

NEW For The Toughest Cleaning Jobs!

rain·X® The Original Pre-Clean 2000™

CREAM CLEANSER

Cleans Glass & Chrome Without Scratching

Removes Bugs, Grime, Stains, Water Spots & Pollutants

GUARANTEED To Be The Best Cleanser Ever!

CAUTION EYE IRRITANT - read back label

300ml (10.0 fl. oz.)

NEW Micro-Polymer Dual-Action Technology

rain·X® The Original SUPER™ GLASS CLEANER

CONCENTRATE

Cleans & Polishes Without Smearing or Streaking

Makes Glass Water & Soil Repellent

Just Add to Water... Makes 64 - 16 oz. Bottles...

Glass Cleaner For Less Than **10¢** Per Bottle

CAUTION: EYE IRRITANT Read Back Label

500 ml (16.93 fl. oz.)

Advanced Micro Glass Coating Te

rain·X® The Original

650

IN RAIN-X

RAIN-X® The Most Trusted Name in Gla-

Unelko Corporation • 14641 N. 74th St. Scotts

at Riverside where Labonte wrapped up his first championship. Hendrick's list of former drivers includes Bodine, Tim Richmond, Brett Bodine, Dick Brooks, Benny Parsons, Darrell Waltrip, Ken Schrader, Greg Sacks, Hut Stricklin, and Ricky Rudd. "It's the best team and the best organization I have ever been with," Labonte said. "Rick Hendrick is one super human being."

Hendrick feels the same way about his drivers. He keeps his distance and allows supervisors to do their work. But when there is a lamb in need, he becomes the shepherd of the flock. Take the Phoenix situation, for example. Labonte slammed the wall during the first practice session and broke a bone in his left hand.

As usual, several in the sport came to the aid of the fallen warrior, and Hendrick was there to provide anything and everything his driver needed.

That's the way it is in Winston Cup racing. Occasionally the fight on the track comes down to fists in the pit area. They fudge on the rule book to gain advantage. Seldom do they pal around together. Sometimes they even wreck each other. But when a competitor falls, they unite like a family to lift him back to his feet.

The wreck on Friday wiped out Labonte's primary car. While Labonte waited, his left hand and wrist wrapped in an ice pack, the crew unloaded the secondary car. Richard Childress, Dale Earnhardt's team owner, wanted to know what he could do to help. Earnhart, Mark Martin and Rusty Wallace talked with crew chief Gary DeHart and each offered to shake the car down. David Green, a NASCAR Grand National division regular at the time, said he would be glad to stand by as a relief driver, but that he didn't have any of his equipment. The Simpson people offered to fit Green with a uniform, shoes and helmet. Ron Hornaday Jr., from the truck racing series, said he would stand by as a relief driver.

Labonte drove the car a few laps of practice and left the track to have xrays made. Meanwhile, Dale Jarrett, 76 points out of the lead and third in the standings, remembered a special

steering wheel constructed for him when he drove for the Joe Gibbs team and had a bone broken in his left hand.

Members of the Gibbs team (which Bobby Labonte now drives for) called the shop in Charlotte and had the steering wheel flown to Phoenix. It was installed in time for Labonte to practice Saturday morning.

Jarrett explained how the steering wheel was constructed. "They made a grip in the wheel. Normally our steering wheels are slick or smooth. This wheel has a grip for your fingers and allows you to use your thumb more than you normally would," he said.

"What I found was I was able to hold the wheel using my fingers more than usual. This allowed me to apply less pressure. It was a little different, and I had to adjust. I don't know which hand Terry uses for the feel of the track," Jarrett said. "I do know he is left handed. I drive more with my right hand, so it wasn't that bad. Knowing Terry, he will do whatever he has to do."

When crewmen installed the wheel in Labonte's car, they had to make the grip smaller because of the swelling in his hand. Labonte wore a red and white glove over a plaster cast. The cast allowed him to grip the wheel with three fingers. The cast had a hard plastic backing with a silicone pad in the palm. According to those who designed it, the primary concern is not holding the wheel, but vibration and steering feedback during the race.

Labonte was treated with a Sport TX stimulator, in which electrodes were placed on the front and back of his hand and adjustable electronic impulses were used to effect pain blocking. The unit was used earlier this year with Dale Earnhardt for treating his shoulder injury after the Talladega accident.

Hendrick was there, standing by Labonte all along. Right after the accident, he called Dr. Walt Beaver in Charlotte to get a recommendation for a doctor in Phoenix. Dr. Beaver recommended Dr. Den Ragaris.

Hendrick also contacted Dr. Terry Trammel in Indianapolis, a noted

sports orthopedic surgeon. If necessary, Hendrick's plan was to fly Labonte by private jet to Indianapolis Friday night for Trammel to analyze the situation and do repairs if necessary. Hendrick then hoped to fly Labonte back Saturday morning.

On Friday night, however, Labonte was at St. Luke's Hospital in Phoenix for a second opinion from a hand specialist.

"You hate to see something like this happen to anyone," Hendrick said, "but Terry is in a heated points race, and we will do everything we can. We have all day Saturday to figure out what we're going to do."

Labonte started 30th in the race. He passed Gordon for ninth place on lap 91 and Geoff Bodine for the lead on lap 196. He led 61 laps of the race and finished third, two positions ahead of Gordon, gaining 15 points in the race for the championship. (Gordon did not lead a lap of the race.) Labonte held a 47 point lead over Gordon after Phoenix.

Hendrick had arranged for Labonte to begin therapy Monday morning with Dr. Beaver at the Miller Orthopedic Clinic in Charlotte. Beaver is an orthopedic doctor with the Carolina Panthers and Charlotte Hornets, and also a big race fan.

Hendrick noted, "We've arranged for an escort to a helicopter. Terry will be lifted out and taken to my plane. He should be home in about four hours to begin therapy Monday morning."

On Hendrick's private jet, Labonte was back in North Carolina in three and a half hours.

"We know it is a spiral fracture," Hendrick continued. "What we don't want is to have it separate again. By Atlanta in a couple of weeks, we should be fine."

Hendrick praised the doctors at Phoenix. "They did a super job with the brace and medication and telling Terry what to do and what not to do with his hand. For what he's gone through, he's fine."

Labonte was "fine" enough to take the Winston Cup title. Gordon was runner-up. Hendrick Motorsports had two titles in a row and an unprecedented, in modern history, 1-2 Winston Cup finish in 1996.

FIRESTONE ACCEPTS THE CHALLENGE... AND YOU WIN!

FIREHAWK
BORN AT INDY. DRIVEN EVERYWHERE.

THE LESSONS WE LEARN ON RACE DAY ARE IN THE TIRES YOU COUNT ON EVERY DAY.

With a record 49 wins at the Indy 500, Firestone knows Indy racing like no other tire company. And if we can develop the kind of quick acceleration, grip and stability required for Indy racing tires, just imagine how well our line of Firehawk street performance radials will perform for you. Firehawk performance tires, including the new, ultra-high performance Firehawk SZ50 with **UNI-T**,™ the **U**ltimate **N**etwork of **I**ntelligent **T**ire **T**echnology, are speed rated from S to Z and specifically engineered for crisp handling and legendary performance. Stop by your local Firestone retailer and check out the complete Firehawk line today. And congratulations to all Indy teams racing on Firestone Firehawk tires. We wish you much success.

Firehawk
Racing Slick

Firehawk
SS10 Street Tire

Firestone
America's Tire Since 1900

uni•T
Ultimate Tire Technology

Original Firehawk
Indy Racing Rain Tire

Firehawk SZ50 Ultra-
High Performance Tire

Indy 500® and Indy® are registered trademarks of the Indianapolis Motor Speedway.

Team of the Year Target/Ganassi Racing
Ganassi's Gamble Pays Off

By Lewis R. Franck

When Chip Ganassi's Target Racing team pulled into spring training at Homestead, Florida, they knew that Ganassi had taken a big gamble on the future. Not even he could have guessed how soon it would pay off.

Essentially, Ganassi gave up the familiar Ford engine program and Goodyear tires to go a new route. The press had questions. What about the new mechanical package and what about new driver, Alex Zanardi of Italy? Could Jimmy Vasser, IndyCar's Most Improved Driver of '95, get into the winner's circle? Some of the answers came quickly, when Vasser won the opening round at Homestead.

Ganassi supplied the background. "Everyone pitched in over the winter to make the changes work. I knew we worked harder," said Ganassi. "Some people said it was just the package - Reynard/Honda/Firestone. From my standpoint, I believe each and every year that we've had a good package. I've come into every year being optimistic, every year feeling I've got a better package than the year before. In '96, as I had in the years past, I felt I had a better shot than in the years before. We, of course, had no way of knowing that when we wheeled into Homestead for spring training what other people had been up to all winter."

What prompted Ganassi to make these bold moves? Most likely his gambler's instinct.

Honda was still just a gathering threat in '95. Everyone knew that the power for superspeedways was there, but what about a whole season of competition. Could they devote sufficient resources to a new team? Turns out they could.

Much of the same philosophy applied to the switch to Firestone. Lots of potential in their first year back in IndyCar competition, 1995.

Could they go head-to-head with the established leader, Goodyear, in '96? Turns out, like Honda, they could.

The next part of the plan was selecting a new co-driver for Vasser. Almost as valuable as the chassis engineering provided by the Reynard team was the advice given by the firm's Rick Gorne and Malcolm Oastler to try out a relatively unknown Italian driver, Alex Zanardi. Zanardi had been highly successful in Reynard Formula 3000 chassis in Europe. Zanardi impressed in the trial and got the job. Ganassi rightly predicted that his transition to Indy cars would be easy.

"I believe that the driving styles of certain drivers are built around the engineering capabilities of a particular chassis manufacturer. Once you master the driving style that a particular manufacturer requires you can carry it through other formulas. That's why you are seeing a lot of guys successful in Reynard Formula 3000 successful in Reynard Indy cars today. They've had the same designer over the years. (Gil de Ferran is another notable example)."

When Vasser began his early season streak by winning three of the year's first four races Ganassi maintains that he wasn't yet thinking about going all the way to the PPG Cup.

"It was interesting. The beginning of the year sort of started and it was nice that we were leading the championship early in the season. I sort of sloughed it off. I knew that we would come under some intense competition as the season went on. Certainly these other people aren't going to lay down and say, 'Okay Chip, see you up front at the Awards Banquet.' One day I woke up and realized that it was our championship to lose. Up until then, leading the points all year didn't really affect me because the competition never sits still. There are

a couple of guys named Michael and Al Jr. and a couple more named Haas and Penske, these guys are not laydowns."

In August, Ganassi first started to think seriously about that coveted championship.

"That sort of came about, around Mid-Ohio. We were leading it the whole time, but some people were quick to point out that Jimmy had some lean races in the middle of the year. Lean, perhaps, but he never failed to finish and was out of the points only once."

Ganassi did have a problem with his new driver, the sort every team owner would love to have. While Vasser was putting in consistent points winning appearances, his new teammate was out-qualifying everybody, burning up the track on race-day and becoming a serious contender for the title, himself.

"As the year came down to the last two or three races, it was difficult for me to straddle. I had one guy leading the championship and a second guy coming on strong who could win it, himself. It was my job to manage the personalities and the motivation of both guys. It helped that Jimmy and Alex do complement each other. Vasser is a more calculating, bring-it-home guy. Zanardi is a hot, fiery guy who will take the chance. (Just like he did successfully at Laguna Seca.)."

There is, of course, more to a team than just the drivers. Take team manager, Tom Anderson, who has been with Ganassi since the beginning. Ganassi says, "He's totally competent and probably the most unselfish person that I know in racing. He's tireless. I wouldn't want to go racing without him."

Is Ganassi content, having found the right formula for '96? Not at all. In typical upbeat fashion he promises, "I'm going to do it again in '97."

Teammates Jimmy Vasser and Alex Zanardi Grab $470,000 in Marlboro Pole Awards and Bonuses

To the victors go the spoils. 1996 champion Jimmy Vasser and his teammate Alex Zanardi, tied for second in PPG Cup points, walked off with the lion's share of the more than half million dollars in '96 Marlboro Pole Awards and Bonuses. They earned it, winning, between the pair, ten of the year's 15 pole positions. (Milwaukee had no official pole winner since qualifying was cancelled.) Vasser's big haul was in the U.S. 500, where he won the $100,000 pole award and $45,000 for winning from the pole. His total for the year was $250,000. Zanardi, the most prolific pole producer of '96 - with six, earned bonuses of $55,000 at Portland, $60,000 at Mid-Ohio, and $45,000 at Monterey. His total was $220,000. Paul Tracy captured two poles, retained his leadership in all-time Marlboro Pole winnings with a $285,000 career total. Gil de Ferran, Scott Pruett, and Andre Ribeiro each scored a single '96 pole, good for $10,000 apiece. For the first time, Marlboro awarded a new Mercedes-Benz E420 sedan to one of the pole winners, each of whom got one Mercedes-Benz car key per pole won. Only one of the keys fit the ignition lock. As might be predicted, Vasser drove off with the E420.

Marlboro's Director of Event Marketing, Ina Broeman, with Jimmy Vasser, winner of $250,000 in '96 Marlboro Pole Awards and bonuses.

Alex Zanardi, the second biggest Marlboro Pole Award and Bonus winner of '96 banked $220,000 for the year.

Marlboro
TEAM PENSKE
Follow us

In most sports athletes hurl a projectile at incredible speeds.

In Indy car racing, you are the projectile.

TOYOTA motorsports

Indy car racing. Man and machine moving at speeds over 180 mph. Toyota is proud to continue sponsorship of the Miami, Long Beach and Monterey Grand Prix. And new for the 1997 CART race season, Nazareth, the U.S. 500 and the California Speedway. Toyota Motorsports. Our minds are always racing.

Drivers

Terry Labonte, A Championship Regained

By Benny Phillips

From the spacious deck of Grizzly Meadows Lodge, you look almost straight down on Yellowstone River. Snow-capped peaks frame the vale appropriately called Paradise Valley.

Grizzly Meadows Lodge is Richard Childress' Montana home. The view came with 600 acres he bought atop a mountain as the site for his nearly 5,000 square foot vacation dwelling. The house, in western mode, is exquisite. For someone steeped in motorsports it is also unique. There is not a single visible trophy, photograph or memento connected with racing. "I don't want anything reminding me of work when I come here," Childress said.

The former race driver, who owns the NASCAR teams Dale Earnhardt and Mike Skinner drive for, has hunted big game over most of North America and in Africa. Several hunting trophies are neatly placed in appropriate areas of the lodge, some in simulation of their environment. Bizarre maybe to some, but Terry Labonte, who works for rival team owner Rick Hendrick, relaxed in the den at Childress's lodge the week after the season finale at Atlanta. He talked about the 1996 racing season.

Labonte had just become the '96 Winston Cup champion. He finished fifth at Atlanta and beat teammate Jeff Gordon by 37 points for the title. Dale Jarrett finished third, and Earnhardt fourth. "Everything in a points race is important," Labonte said, "but when I try to analyze the year, I guess the two races where our performance helped most toward winning the title were Martinsville and Phoenix. Maybe I should turn that around and say those are the events that frighten me most when I think about the season. We could have lost the championship in either race."

Labonte was 76 points behind Gordon before the Martinsville race, which was six events from the end of the season. Gordon qualified tenth and Labonte 11th. Both moved near the front of the field early in the race, but Labonte's car lost a clutch rod on lap 120. On a pit stop, members of the crew jumped into the car and vice-gripped the clutch back in place. It held until the last caution. On the restart the device fell off, but Labonte still finished second to Gordon, holding off Bobby Hamilton, John Andretti and Rick Mast. When the clutch rod fell off, he pitted and lost a lap. Back on the track, Labonte first passed Gordon and then Hamilton, the race leader, to unlap himself. Then he chased down and passed Andretti for second place on lap 448. He tried to catch Gordon the final 52 laps.

"Jeff won the race and I finished second, but under the circumstances I could have just as well finished tenth, 12th or on back," Labonte said. "That clutch rod is a trophy. It could have cost us the championship. That's just one of the reasons I can't say enough about our crew. Those guys were magnificent."

Gordon won the race and finished one position ahead of Labonte and picked up five points, leading by 81 points with five races left. Dale Jarrett trailed by 162 points.

Gordon won the following week at North Wilkesboro and Labonte finished fifth. Labonte did not lead a lap. Gordon gained five bonus points for leading and another five for leading the most laps. He posted his fourth win in the last five races and his tenth and final victory of the season. Gordon gained 30 points on Labonte and led by 111 going to Charlotte.

Charlotte in early October turned out to be the break Labonte needed. He recognizes this and realizes he could not have won the championship without such a turn of luck, but ranks Martinsville and Phoenix ahead of Charlotte in the chase for the title because those were the two races where he could have lost it all.

"Charlotte was important, very important," Labonte said. "Without what happened at Charlotte we would not have won the championship, but I guess I look more at where we could have lost it than where we might have won it."

Labonte led 129 of 334 laps and won the 500-miler at Charlotte. Gordon experienced mechanical failure to finish 31st in the 43 car field. Labonte gained 110 points and trailed by a single point as the circuit moved to Rockingham. Labonte finished third and Gordon 12th at Rockingham. Labonte headed for Phoenix, the penultimate round, with a 32 point lead.

Just minutes after the track opened for practice in the Valley of the Sun, the throttle hung on Labonte's car. He crashed, breaking a bone in his left hand. He tried to drive a backup car with his hand broken and was going to qualify the car, but a dust storm blew in and postponed time trials. Doctors at a Phoenix hospital worked with the hand overnight and prepared a splint of sorts so he could qualify Saturday and race Sunday. Bobby Labonte won the pole, and Terry qualified 30th. Gordon started the race 19th.

Though wounded, Terry led 61 laps and finished third. Gordon finished fifth, and Labonte gained 15 points. He headed for Atlanta and the season finale with a 47 point lead. "With my hand broken and all, I would have settled for 12th place at Phoenix and gone on to the next race," Labonte said.

"Another thing about our third place finish at Phoenix was that it pumped our team up," he said. "I think members of our team were at a season high going to Atlanta. It was like all of a sudden they knew we could win the championship. I have heard football coaches say that it makes a lot of difference at what point of the season a team peaks. Believe me there is something to this. We peaked at the perfect time."

Labonte finished fifth, Gordon third. Brother Bobby Labonte won the race. Terry won the title by 37 points. Anywhere along the line, a difference of eight positions, or even six positions with bonus points thrown in, could have shifted the championship to Gordon.

"You can always look at what could have happened, and sometimes the little things make you tremble," Childress told Labonte.

Childress, Earnhardt's team owner in six of seven championship runs, can relate to where titles are won and lost. "The main thing is to jerk off the rear-view mirror, throw it away, and don't look back," Childress said. "What's behind you right now is not important. Just have a good time, enjoy being the champion and look to next year."

And how did this Labonte-Childress rendezvous occur within a few days of the championship? Were big moves about in NASCAR land? Not at all. The hunting trip, planned nearly a year ago, brought together a few friends at Grizzly Meadow Lodge. Labonte hunted in Big Sky Country in 1995 and was telling stories about the trip. Childress listened and then explained he had a vacation home there. "Let's go next year (1996) and we'll stay at my place."

Arrangements were made and at the time nobody had any idea how the season would turn out. It could not have turned out to be a better holiday for Labonte. He won the championship, and on the day he wrapped up the title in the season finale at Atlanta, his brother Bobby won the race and the Labonte clan had a lot to celebrate.

Bob Labonte, Terry and Bobby's father, never forced his sons to race, but was always available to turn the

wrenches if they were willing. Bob grew up in Maine and left home at an early age to join the Navy. While with Uncle Sam, he was stationed at Corpus Christi, Texas, where he met Martha Wright. Soon they were married, and Terry and Bobby followed. Terry started with quarter-midgets. Later Bobby started with go-karts. Bob would take Terry and his quarter-midget car to shopping center parking lots on Sunday afternoon. He would take along a long string of gallon milk jugs while Bob clocked every lap with a stopwatch.

At age 17, when most kids still are trying to decide whether they want to be a rock 'n' roll drummer or an astronaut, Terry Labonte was uprooting the establishment of short track racing, reeling in Saturday night legends from Corpus Christi to San Antonio to Houston to Shreveport. He drove a runaway locomotive in 63 events in 1974 (when he was 17) and won 54 of them. His crew consisted of his father Bob, who called the shots, and a few of Bob's friends.

When you come from 250 miles away and wear out local favorites, fans have a tendency to turn against you like a pack of dawg pound dogs. Before Terry was 18, he knew what it was like to have soft drink cups and beer bottles bounce from the hood of his race car as he did the victory lap, his left hand holding the checkered flag out the window.

He learned to remain calm, to bring the car back to the pits where Bob and friends waited and watched. If anybody threw anything at Bob and crew, it was from long distance.

Sometimes a winner is the best thing promoters have going. Labonte was winning so often that fans packed the grandstands, half to see him lose, half to see him win.

It was ironic that in the week last spring when Terry brought an 18 season, 513 race consecutive start streak to Martinsville Speedway to break Richard Petty's record, Bob would remember that a no-show in Houston led to one of his son's biggest breaks. "We were supposed to race at Myers Speedway in Houston," Bob said. "It is 240 miles

one way from Corpus Christi to Houston, and we just flat didn't have the money to make the trip. We wanted to go, and everybody was mad because we couldn't go. So, we all went down on the beach and had a cookout. "The break came Monday when Ed Hamblin, the promoter from Houston, called. "Ed wanted to know why we weren't there," Bob said. "I told him we didn't have the money, that we would have been there if we could have afforded it." Hamblin called his friend Billy Hagan, a Louisiana entrepreneur. Hagan called the Labontes and sponsored the team the rest of the season with his Stratograph company.

Hagan, with Stratograph sponsorship, brought Labonte into Winston Cup racing. Labonte's first event was the Southern 500 at Darlington in 1978. He finished fourth. Two years later he won at Darlington, posting his first Winston Cup victory. As Labonte stood in victory circle that Labor Day afternoon, tired and showing very little enthusiasm, it was suggested that the guy needed a fast injection of emotion if he was going to make it in this sport.

Labonte never changed but he has made it big in NASCAR - two championships plus nearly 20 victories and enough money to take over the total mortgage payments of most small towns. He has done it his way, and his way is the quiet way - a friendly smile and a gentle wave. He's just the same as he was the day he arrived on the circuit. He's comfortable any day of the week in blue jeans, and is more at ease around friends he picked rather than friends who picked him.

He *is* bolder on the track, and will lend you his front bumper if you mess with his back bumper.

He was glad to have the Petty record breaking behind him. Happy that the media moved on to something else and forgot who broke what record. Labonte was nice about it, but didn't think it was all that big a deal, although he filled more than 250 media requests surrounding his pursuit of Petty's record, including throwing the first baseball out at

IF THIS IS YOUR LIFE, THIS IS YOUR NETWORK.

TNN HAS MORE LIVE MOTORSPORTS THAN *ANY* OTHER NETWORK.

TNN MOTOR SPORTS

COVERS THE SPORT, NOT JUST THE RACE.

Camden Yards in Baltimore prior to the Orioles-Red Sox game. "The interest was pretty amazing. I guess I realize now that anyone who goes out and does his job well for 17 years without missing too many beats is making a statement about consistency. That's pretty important in any job." he said.

Labonte was lucky to break Petty's record, but, of course, Petty was lucky to set the record. So many things happen along the way.

Take the final race of the 1982 season. Had the race been any other time, Labonte would not own the record. When he opened his eyes that autumn day in '82, Labonte realized he was a patient in an ambulance going somewhere. He hurt all over. He figured it was bad, although he didn't try to analyze the extent of his injuries. He did notice a sympathetic expression on the face of the nurse who worked feverishly over his motionless body.

"Am I going to die?" Labonte asked. He remembers the look of fear on the nurse's face as she turned away and refused to answer the question.

Labonte spent the next week in a California hospital, nursing a broken leg, a broken right foot, broken ribs and a broken nose. He had survived a devastating head-on crash with the notorious wall at the end of the long backstretch at Riverside Raceway.

Riverside was the final race of the 1982 season. Labonte was running 165 mph at the end of the backstretch, approaching turn nine, a sweeping right turn where maximum speed was about 85. When he pumped the brake pedal to make the turn, the pedal went to the floorboard and stayed. He had no brakes and no time. The front of his race car chewed on the wall like a hungry termite and lost. There was nothing left but a heap of scrap metal, barely too large to haul home on the bed of a pickup truck. Had the wreck occurred at any time other than the last race of the season, he would not have broken Petty's record of 513 consecutive events.

"I was in no shape to race the next weekend," Labonte said. "I hurt all over, I had a cast on one leg and a brace of sorts on the other."

It was the low point of Labonte's career. "I was about ready to quit racing. I think I would have if my wife Kim had asked me to hang it up. But she never mentioned it. I'm glad she didn't."

Labonte has not missed a Winston Cup race since he began his rookie season at the now-defunct Riverside Raceway on January 14, 1979. Labonte ran five races in 1978, but his consecutive streak did not begin until the next year.

Petty's 513 race streak began in February 1971 and extended until March 26, 1989, when he failed to qualify for the weather delayed 400 at Richmond Raceway.

Labonte won the North Wilkesboro race last spring on the day he tied Petty's record at Martinsville. It was not all that much to Labonte, but he played the role.

The role he likes is the role of champion. That one he will play throughout the 1997 season. The '97 season will, however, have to go some to top the previous year.

For example there was the old man who said he didn't care much for sports, but that he did watch stock car racing on TV now and again. "Tell you what," he said, "wasn't much to last racing season, but when it was over and them Labonte brothers pulled their cars side-by-side in Atlanta and drove around the track, that sort of put a big lump in a fellow's throat. Fact is, it was about the most emotional thing I've seen in sports in a long, long time."

Immediately after the checkered flag, the brothers - Terry on the inside and Bobby on the outside - had driven slowly around Atlanta Speedway to the plaudits of a stand up crowd.

There were other emotional moments, too. Ernie Irvan won in July at Loudon, New Hampshire, his first victory since the crash at Michigan in 1994 which nearly took his life.

Geoff Bodine won in August at Watkins Glen in front of a hometown crowd, his first win in nearly two years.

Dale Earnhardt survived the worst wreck of his career at Talladega in July when Ernie Irvan got into the side of Sterling Marlin and turned Marlin's left front into Earnhardt's right rear. This turned Earnhardt, who was leading the race, into the frontstretch grandstand wall. The violent crash left Earnhardt with a broken sternum and fractured collar bone. Bruised and aching, Earnhardt qualified his car the next week at Indianapolis. He started the race for the points, and Mike Skinner took over as a relief driver on lap six. Earnhardt was credited with a 15th place finish. The following week, Earnhardt captured the pole position on the twisting road course at Watkins Glen and drove the distance of the race to finish sixth.

Dale Jarrett won the big money races of the year. He won the Daytona 500 for the second time, then won the Coca-Cola 600 at Charlotte, followed by the Brickyard 400 at Indianapolis.

Michael Waltrip drove the Wood Brothers Ford to a fifth place finish in the Winston Open. Fifth in the Open turned out to be the last position to earn a spot in the Winston Select at Charlotte in May. But when the final ten laps of the all-star race unfolded, Waltrip grabbed the lead and led to the finish.

Bruton Smith and Bob Bahre closed the doors to Winston Cup racing at North Wilkesboro Speedway when they purchased the track and whisked away the dates, Smith taking the spring date to his new Texas track and Bahre moving the fall date to his New Hampshire track. Jeff Gordon won the last scheduled race there in late September.

Yet, when you consider all the dramatic moments of the year, none surpass an October afternoon in Phoenix. Bobby Hamilton put the Richard Petty owned Pontiac in victory circle. Hamilton posted his first Winston Cup victory and the first for a Petty owned car since July of 1984 when Petty himself won the 200th race of his career.

Steve Swope

1 Consistency and Courage... **Terry Labonte** transformed two victories and unsurpassed mental toughness into a second Winston Cup Championship. (4657 Winston Cup points)

Things moved right along to the annual awards banquet in New York where Labonte collected more than $1.5 million from R.J. Reynolds for his title run. For the year his total winnings amounted to nearly $4 million.

On the business side of racing, several drivers made changes during the year.

Ken Schrader left Hendrick Motorsports to join Andy Petree and the No. 33 Chevrolet team. Ricky Craven left Hedrick Motorsports and replaced Schrader at Hendrick Motorsports.

Kyle Petty started his own team. When he left team owner Felix Sabates, Sabates announced he would run three teams in 1997. He moved in Robby Gordon from Indy cars to replace Petty. He purchased Joe Nemechek's team and hired him as a driver. He also signed Wally Dallenbach to drive a limited schedule.

Rick Mast left the Richard Jackson team to join the Butch Mock Ford operation. It turns out to be a switch. Morgan Shepherd, Mock's driver in '96, will driver for Jackson in 1997.

Derrike Cope left the Bobby Allison team and will drive for a new team owned by Nelson Bowers.

Richard Childress is operating two teams in '97 with Earnhardt in one car and Mike Skinner in the other.

Robert Pressley left the Andy Petree team and joined Diamond Ridge. Steve Grissom, who once drove for Diamond Ridge, went to the Larry Hedrick team where Craven was in '96.

David Green and Chad Little moved up with their teams from NASCAR's Grand National division.

It turned out to be a competitive season, too. Earnhardt won the pole and Irvan outside front row for the Daytona 500. Jarrett, however, won the Busch Clash with Sterling Marlin second, Earnhardt third, Terry Labonte fourth and Schrader fifth.

Earnhardt and Irvan won the 125-mile qualifying races on Thursday prior to the 500. Irvan led all 50 laps of the second 125 while Marlin led

the first 29 laps of the first race before Earnhardt took command and led the last 21 laps.

In the 500, it was Jarrett winning for the second time with Earnhardt finishing second for the fourth time. Schrader finished third, Mark Martin fourth and Jeff Burton fifth.

Earnhardt came back the next week and won Rockingham and Jarrett finished second this time. Terry Labonte won the pole and led the most laps, but finished 34th when mechanical failure sidelined him for the second week in a row. In the final laps of the race, Earnhardt and Bobby Hamilton got together while racing for the lead. Hamilton wrecked, and it started the first controversy of the year.

Gordon won at Richmond, and Jarrett finished second to take the points lead.

Earnhardt came right back to win Atlanta. In a twist of bad luck, Jeff Burton, who was second in the points standings, did not qualify fast enough to make the race and had to go home.

Gordon won the next two races, Darlington and Bristol. Then Terry Labonte won North Wilkesboro from the pole to tie Richard Petty's record of starting 513 consecutive races.

The next week at Martinsville, Labonte broke the record while Rusty Wallace drove to victory.

Sterling Marlin won at Talladega, and Ricky Craven survived one of the wildest rides of the year when he was involved in a turn two crash.

Wallace posted his second win of the season, taking the checkered flag at Sears Point.

The series then moved to Charlotte where Michael Waltrip won the Winston Select, and then Jarrett captured the 600. Gordon won two more straight, taking Dover and then Pocono. Wallace also won in June, sweeping Michigan.

Meanwhile, Loy Allen, injured at Rockingham, returned to the bucket seat at Pocono, and Dick Trickle replaced Mike Wallace in the Junie Donlavey Ford ride.

Also, Jarrett broke a leg and some ribs in practice at Pocono, but

started the race only to have mechanical failure.

Marlin dominated the July 4th race in Daytona, where Dave Marcis started his 800th career race. Greg Sacks also replaced Steve Grissom, with the Diamond Ridge team.

The next week, Irvan won at Loudon. Wallace took the second race at Pocono.

Earnhardt set the pace at Talladega and was leading on lap 118 when the most spectacular wreck of the year occurred.

Earnhardt led the way with Marlin second and Irvan third. Marlin was outside Earnhardt. Irvan followed Earnhardt, but moved up and tagged the left rear of Marlin's car. This turned Marlin's front into Earnhardt's right rear which turned Earnhardt almost straight into the walll. Gordon won the race and Earnhardt, the points leader at the time, finished 28th.

Jarrett beat Irvan the next week at Indianapolis, and then Bodine won at Watkins Glen after Earnhardt won the pole. Jarrett took the checkered flag at Michigan, and Wallace won the night race at Bristol.

Jarrett arrived in Darlington for the Southern 500 with a chance at the Winston Million bonus, available to any driver who wins three of NASCAR's four big races. Jarrett won Daytona and Charlotte. He captured the pole at Darlington, but got into some oil and hit the wall on lap 46. He never ran well after that, and Gordon won the race.

Irvan won his second race of the year at Richmond. Jeremy Mayfield and John Andretti switched rides for the rest of the season.

Gordon took the next three straight - Dover, Martinsville and North Wilkesboro - and he seemed headed for a second straight championship, but Labonte would have the final word.

Labonte won Charlotte, and two weeks later Ricky Rudd won at Rockingham to keep his win streak alive for 13 straight years. Then came Phoenix and finally Atlanta. What a dramatic year. No wonder the old man got a lump in his throat.

Nigel Kinrade

2 Ten Victories Not Enough... **Jeff Gordon** won twice as many races as anybody else but a single disastrous weekend cost him a repeat title. (4620 Winston Cup points)

3 500 Mile Master... **Dale Jarrett** captured three of the year's biggest races, four in all, for a great year at the bank. (4568 Winston Cup points)

Nigel Kinrade

4 Accident Victim... **Dale Earnhardt** won twice, was in contention for an eighth championship until a crash, not of his making, took the edge off his campaign. (4327 Winston Cup points)

Nigel Kinrade

5 Front Runner... **Mark Martin** needed only a bit of luck to convert one of his 14 top five finishes into victory. (4278 Winston Cup points) He's shown with team owner Jack Roush, one of the sport's savviest.

Nigel Kinrade

6 Record Intact... **Ricky Rudd** now has 13 years in the record book with at least a single victory in each. At midseason his outlook was bleak. (3845 Winston Cup points)

7 Five First Places... **Rusty Wallace** won on every kind of track that NASCAR runs, was second only to Gordon in the victory column. Mechanical problems hurt. (3717 Winston Cup points)

Nigel Kinrade

8 Still Strong on the Superspeedways... **Sterling Marlin** won twice, maintained his reputation as a force on the big tracks. (3682 Winston Cup points)

9 Victory at Last... **Bobby Hamilton** had come close before, but his win at Phoenix served notice of brighter horizons in '97 for the Richard Petty/STP/Pontiac combination. (3639 Winston Cup points)

Nigel Kinrade

Swedish Fan Designs New Paint Scheme for Petty's '97 STP Pontiac

"It's real neat," says Richard Petty of the award-winning paint scheme for the '97 edition of his famed STP Pontiac. "I like it and so do Bobby Hamilton and the crew." Surprise winner of the contest to be the designer of Petty's new racing color scheme was 34 year old Lars Svensson of Helinsburg, Sweden, who has seen several Winston Cup races and is founder of the Swedish NASCAR Club. Equally surprising to Dave Berlin, Motorsports Manager at STP, the contest's sponsors, was the number of entries. The total came to more than 6000 from all 50 states and nine foreign countries. Driver Hamilton added, "It will be fun driving a car designed by someone who lives so far away." Winner Svensson will be the envy of his fellow club members, STP is providing him and three friends with an all expense paid trip to the Daytona 500, along with his $1,000 honorarium for winning the "Design the King's Car" contest. Petty and Hamilton presided at the unveiling ceremony in Charlotte and hope to improve on a banner '96 season.

Steve Swope

10 Comeback Completed... **Ernie Irvan** proved that, once again, he was back in NASCAR's elite contingent with not one, but two wins, and 12 top five finishes. (3632 Winston Cup points)

Steve Swope

11 A Single Victory... **Bobby Labonte's** win, combined with brother Terry's title, made Atlanta a family festival. (3590 Winston Cup points)

Nigel Kinrade

12 Up Five Places... **Ken Schrader** moved into Winston Cup's top dozen but was still short of victory circle.   (3540 Winston Cup points)

13 Showing Potential... **Jeff Burton** scored six top five finishes, 12 top tens.   (3538 Winston Cup points)

14 Even Keel... **Michael Waltrip** essentially matched his '95 season.   (3535 Winston Cup points)

Nigel Kinrade

Nigel Kinrade

15 Getting Better... **Jimmy Spencer** gained eleven places over his rank last season.
(3476 Winston Cup points)

Nigel Kinrade

16 Out of the Top Ten... **Ted Musgrave** dropped out of the elite top ten. (3466 Winston Cup points)

Dan Bianchi

17 Surprise Winner... **Geoff Bodine's** single victory capped a season otherwise much the same as its predecessor. (3218 Winston Cup points)

Nigel Kinrade

18 Edging Upward... **Rick Mast** moved up three places on the Winston Cup chart. (3190 Winston Cup points)

Nigel Kinrade

19 Still in the Top 20 ... **Morgan Shepherd** slipped in the points standings, retained top 20 status and his loyal fans.   (3133 Winston Cup points)

Nigel Kinrade

20 New to the Top Five... **Ricky Craven** posted three top five finishes, is knocking on the door to victory.   (3078 Winston Cup points)

1996 NASCAR Winston Cup Points

POS.	DRIVER	POINTS	STARTS	WINS	TOP-5	TOP-10	MONEY WON
1	TERRY LABONTE	4657	31	2	21	24	$1,939,213
2	JEFF GORDON	4620	31	10	21	24	2,484,518
3	DALE JARRETT	4568	31	4	17	21	2,343,750
4	DALE EARNHARDT	4327	31	2	13	17	1,725,396
5	MARK MARTIN	4278	31	0	14	23	1,550,555
6	RICKY RUDD	3845	31	1	5	16	1,213,373
7	RUSTY WALLACE	3717	31	5	8	18	1,296,912
8	STERLING MARLIN	3682	31	2	5	10	1,315,050
9	BOBBY HAMILTON	3639	31	1	3	11	954,625
10	ERNIE IRVAN	3632	31	2	12	16	1,480,167
11	BOBBY LABONTE	3590	31	1	5	14	1,362,415
12	KEN SCHRADER	3540	31	0	3	10	979,287
13	JEFF BURTON	3538	30	0	6	12	729,852
14	MICHAEL WALTRIP	3535	31	0	1	11	1,063,825
15	JIMMY SPENCER	3476	31	0	2	9	937,255
16	TED MUSGRAVE	3466	31	0	2	7	868,555
17	GEOFF BODINE	3218	31	1	2	6	937,970
18	RICK MAST	3190	31	0	1	5	835,532
19	MORGAN SHEPHERD	3133	31	0	1	5	638,597
20	RICKY CRAVEN	3078	31	0	3	5	865,362
21	JOHNNY BENSON	3004	30	0	1	6	893,580
22	HUT STRICKLIN	2854	31	0	1	1	601,555
23	LAKE SPEED	2834	31	0	0	2	789,175
24	BRETT BODINE	2814	30	0	0	1	741,716
25	WALLY DALLENBACH JR.	2786	30	0	1	3	794,501
26	JEREMY MAYFIELD	2721	30	0	2	2	592,853
27	KYLE PETTY	2696	28	0	0	2	689,041
28	KENNY WALLACE	2694	30	0	0	2	457,665
29	DARRELL WALTRIP	2657	31	0	0	2	740,185
30	BILL ELLIOTT	2627	24	0	0	6	706,506
31	JOHN ANDRETTI	2621	30	0	2	3	688,511
32	ROBERT PRESSLEY	2485	30	0	2	3	690,465
33	WARD BURTON	2411	27	0	0	4	873,619
34	JOE NEMECHEK	2391	29	0	0	2	666,247
35	DERRIKE COPE	2374	29	0	0	3	675,781
36	DICK TRICKLE	2131	26	0	0	1	404,927
37	BOBBY HILLIN JR.	2128	26	0	0	0	382,724
38	DAVE MARCIS	2047	27	0	0	0	435,177
39	STEVE GRISSOM	1188	13	0	1	2	314,983
40	TODD BODINE	991	10	0	0	1	198,525
41	MIKE WALLACE	799	11	0	0	0	169,082
42	GREG SACKS	710	9	0	0	0	207,755
43	ELTON SAWYER	705	9	0	0	0	129,618
44	CHAD LITTLE	627	9	0	0	0	164,752
45	LOY ALLEN	603	9	0	0	0	130,667
46	GARY BRADBERRY	591	9	0	0	0	155,785
47	MIKE SKINNER	529	5	0	0	0	65,850
48	JEFF PURVIS	328	4	0	0	0	91,127
49	JEFF GREEN	247	4	0	0	0	46,875
50	RANDY MacDONALD	228	3	0	0	0	33,910

NASCAR Winston Cup Race 1
Daytona 500
Daytona International Speedway
Daytona Beach, Florida
February 18, 1996
200 Laps, 500 Miles

DALE JARRETT DOES IT AGAIN WINS DAYTONA 500

Actually, a pair of Dales did it again in the Daytona 500. Dale Jarrett won for the second time, this time in the Quality Care/Ford Credit Ford. Dale Earnhardt didn't for the 18th time in a row. Not that Earnhardt did not try. He put his familiar black GM Goodwrench Chevrolet on the pole and led the field on five occasions, the last of which ended on lap 176. At this point, Jarrett, the leader on four previous tours took over and edged Earnhardt to the checker by a slim .12 of a second. Ernie Irvan in the Texaco-Havoline Ford, the second fastest qualifier, rocketed into the lead at the start, stayed in front for two laps, was never again a major factor. Sterling Marlin (who took the 1994 and 1995 Daytona 500s), in the Kodak Chevrolet, was a strong contender from his third starting position, led a couple of laps (77 through 79), and was sidelined with engine failure two laps later. Derrike Cope, the 1990 Daytona 500 winner, and Jeff Gordon, the current Winston Cup titleholder, were even earlier retirees, completing only 53 and 13 laps, respectively. Ken Schrader, the fourth fastest qualifier in the Budweiser Chevrolet, had a good day, leading twice and finishing third. Terry Labonte, a strong contender in the early going, faded to 24th at the end. Over the last 24 laps it was all Jarrett and Earnhardt, with Jarrett out in front and unfazed by any of the intense pressure generated by Earnhardt, a master in countdown situations.

Nigel Kinrade

Big Day for Ford... Ford Customer Service Division General Manager, Ron Goldsberry and Edsel Ford, President of Ford Credit, flank Thunderbird driver, Dale Jarrett, in the winner's circle at the Daytona 500, crown jewel of NASCAR racing.

Nigel Kinrade

Nigel Kinrade

NASCAR Winston Cup Race 2
Goodwrench Service 400
North Carolina Motor Speedway
Rockingham, North Carolina
February 25, 1996
393 Laps, 400 Miles

DALE EARNHARDT BOUNCES BACK, WINS AT ROCKINGHAM

The two Dales squared off again at Rockingham. This time Earnhardt prevailed; runner-up Jarrett didn't even get a last lap run on the winner. The final two laps proceeded under caution as a result of Bobby Hillin's encounter with the wall. Terry Labonte had a great outing underway, leading the first 88 laps from the pole in his Kellogg's Chevrolet and forcing the pace until his engine expired on lap 235, while again in the lead, his fifth stint up front. Ricky Craven came from far back to claim third place in the Kodiak Chevrolet. Jeff Gordon had another unhappy day behind the wheel of his DuPont Chevrolet, after qualifying second fastest; engine failure again after only 134 laps of the 393 scheduled.

Bobby Hamilton demonstrated new speed in the STP Pontiac, gaining the lead for the third time on lap 344, but bowing out on lap 383 after a tangle with Wally Dallenbach's Ford. Ricky Rudd brought the Tide Ford home fourth to nail down third place in the Winston Cup standings at this early stage. The two Dales ended up tied in the Winston Cup standings each with a victory and a second place. There was, however, that little matter of a $276,931 differential in first place prize money in Jarrett's favor due to the generous payday that Daytona 500 winners earn.

NASCAR Winston Cup Race 3
Pontiac Excitement 400
Richmond International Speedway
Richmond, Virginia
March 3, 1996
400 Laps, 300 Miles

JEFF GORDON GRABS RICHMOND WIN

True champion that he is, Jeff Gordon shrugged off his abysmal luck in the new season's first two events, and posted his first victory of 1996 at Richmond. Gordon nailed down the outside pole in qualifying, was in contention all day, took command from Jeff Burton on lap 351. At the end, the 1995 Winston Cup champion had a .56 of a second margin on Dale Jarrett, up from the 11th qualifying position in his Quality Care Ford. Ted Musgrave notched third place. Gordon teammate, Terry Labonte was on the pole, could hold the lead only three laps before giving way to Bobby Hamilton, the third fastest qualifier, in the STP Pontiac. Labonte eventually slipped to eighth place while Hamilton, who was bumped by Kmart/Little Caesar's driver John Andretti in a late race incident, was lucky to finish sixth. Andretti continued to bump Hamilton after the checker, incurring a $2,000 NASCAR fine for conduct detrimental to the sport. Burton's strong fourth place in the Pontiac Excitement 400 earned him the second spot in Winston Cup points behind leader Jarrett. Perennial "man to beat" Dale Earnhardt had a dismal day which ended in 31st place.

NASCAR Winston Cup Race 4
Purolator 500
Atlanta Motor Speedway
Hampton, Georgia
March 10, 1996
328 Laps, 500 Miles

DALE EARNHARDT, WITH LUCK, BACK ON TOP IN ATLANTA

Tough enough on his own, Dale Earnhardt normally needs no help to win races. To take his eighth career win at Atlanta, he graciously accepted a big boost from Lady Luck. Going for their last pit stops, Terry Labonte's Kellogg's Chevrolet held a six car length advantage over Earnhardt's GM Goodwrench Chevrolet. When both got back out on the track, Earnhardt was ahead by about five seconds. A jammed lug nut during Labonte's pit stop made the difference. The mishap cost Labonte any chance at the top spot, but didn't keep him out of the runner-up slot. Jeff Gordon in the DuPont car took third place, further evidence that he and his crew were back in form. The surprise polesitter, Johnny Benson, in the Pennzoil Pontiac, was outsprinted at the start by Labonte, finished near the bottom of the chart. Texaco's Ernie Irvan, coming from far back, was a strong fourth place finisher. Jeff Burton, in second place in the Winston Cup standings after the first three races, failed to make the field. He took the disappointment, a measure of how competitive the '96 Winston Cup fields are, in stride.

NASCAR Winston Cup Race 5
Transouth Financial 400
Darlington Raceway
Darlington, South Carolina
March 24, 1996
293 Laps, 400 Miles

JEFF GORDON DELIVERS THE WIN, RIVALS RUN OUT OF FUEL

Better fuel management was the key to Jeff Gordon's Darlington victory as he and Dale Jarrett dueled in the final stages of the Transouth Financial 400. The late race drama was set up by a caution flag on lap 220 of the 293 scheduled, tempting drivers to try and go the remaining 73 without refueling again. Gordon, in the lead on lap 287, made it to the checker. Race long rival Jarrett didn't, running out of precious high octane fuel on the last lap. His fate had already been sealed seven laps earlier when a slower car squeezed him into the wall, causing a tire rub and a subsequent loss of speed. Rusty Wallace and Bobby Hamilton were among the others plagued with fuel problems. Wallace managed to take fourth place, behind Bobby Labonte and Ricky Craven and ahead of Terry Labonte. Surprise polesitter Ward Burton in the MBNA Pontiac could manage only seven laps in the lead, before giving way to Gordon. An accident on lap 137 ended his day. Dale Earnhardt had an undistinguished day, finishing 14th, he left the track immediately. Despite being classified 15th today by the officials, Jarrett led the Winston Cup points with 783, Gordon moved up to ninth in the totals with 653.

Nigel Kinrade

Nigel Kinrade

NASCAR Winston Cup Race 6
Food City 500
Bristol International Raceway
Bristol, Tennessee
March 31, 1996
500 Laps, 266.5 Miles

JEFF GORDON'S WINNING RAMPAGE CONTINUES AT BRISTOL

Making up for his dismal season start, Winston Cup Champion Jeff Gordon made Bristol his third win in his last four outings. Once again the finish was under caution, occasioned by Darrell Waltrip's excursion into the wall, but Gordon had already asserted his dominance. Second finisher Terry Labonte, the second fastest qualifier, was the runner-up, while polesitter Mark Martin, in the Valvoline Ford, earned the third slot at the finish. Rusty Wallace, in the Miller Ford, had a long run out front but ended up fifth

just behind Dale Earnhardt. Earnhardt muscled his way into the front running contingent from far back without, however, ever taking the lead. Dale Jarrett, sixth today, retained his lead in the Winston Cup standings, ahead of Earnhardt and Rudd. Gordon, nowhere at the beginning of the year, was making his presence felt; annexed sixth place in the standings.

NASCAR Winston Cup Race 7
First Union 400
North Wilkesboro Speedway
North Wilkesboro, North Carolina
April 14, 1996
400 Laps, 250 Miles

TERRY LABONTE ON TOP IN WILKESBORO

On the pole for the third time of the new season, Terry Labonte

hustled his Kellogg's Chevrolet to the front, stayed there for the first 56 laps of the 400 scheduled at North Wilkesboro, and, just as neatly, ran out the last 26 laps firmly in charge. Not that teammate Jeff Gordon, in the DuPont Chevrolet, who started back in the 17th slot, didn't make it interesting. He was only .239 of a second behind at the end. Dale Earnhardt came from even further back, 26th at the start, to finish third. Elton Sawyer, the surprise second fastest qualifier, faded to 32nd at the end. In the lead at five different stages of the race, Terry Labonte was clearly the class of the field. At day's end he owned 1004 Winston Cup points, the third highest total after Jarrett, 1063, and Dale Earnhardt, 1061. In notching his first win of the year and topping the Busch Pole Award standings, Labonte clearly indicated that he must be considered a serious contender for the '96 championship.

NASCAR Winston Cup Race 8
Goody's Headache Powder 500
Martinsville Speedway
Martinsville, Virginia
April 21, 1996
500 Laps, 263 Miles

RUSTY WALLACE, THE MONARCH OF MARTINSVILLE

Shut out of the winner's circle so far in 1996, Rusty Wallace came roaring back in style to put his Miller Ford squarely into checkered flag territory at Martinsville. On one mid-race streak he led for 128 consecutive laps, a considerable feat on Martinsville's tight half mile. Ernie Irvan sent a clear message that he and his Texaco Ford, too, are about ready for victory circle, hustling into the runner-up slot from next to the back row at the start. Jeff Gordon, now clearly back in form after a slow season start, earned the third slot at the finish, two places up on rival Dale Earnhardt, in fifth place at the

end. Jeremy Mayfield, in the RCA Ford, had a good day at the office with a fifth place finish. Kyle Petty, showing flashes of his old form in the Coors Pontiac was the second fastest qualifier, led for 66 laps early in the contest but finished far down in 30th place.

Earnhardt, 1221, Gordon, 1145, and Dale Jarrett, 1139, luckless in 29th place today, remain atop the Winston Cup point standings.

NASCAR Winston Cup Race 9
Winston Select 500
Talladega Superspeedway
Talladega, Alabama
April 28, 1996
188 Laps, 500 Miles

STERLING MARLIN TAKES TALLADEGA

Sterling Marlin loves superspeedways and 500 mile races. So does Dale Jarrett. Not unexpectedly,

these two masters of the high banks and their mandatory restrictor plates fought it out to an incredibly close finish. Marlin prevailed by a mere .22 of a second in a classic long distance encounter. Marlin out jumped polesitter Ernie Irvan to lead the first two laps, gave way to Jarrett and Dale Earnhardt in turn, before Irvan wrested back the lead, only to fall to the 31st slot at the end. To the fans' delight, there were 24 lead changes among 14 drivers. Earnhardt had one other sojourn in the lead, finished third, but was unable to put a meaningful move on the top two at the end. Jeff Gordon took the lead twice but became an accident victim after 141 laps. This misfortune vaulted Gordon's teammate, Terry Labonte into third place in the Winston Cup standings with 1265, behind Earnhardt, 1391, and Jarrett, 1314. Gordon's misfortunes dropped him to the fourth ranking with 1214. There were ten other drivers whose days were cut short by accidents, including such front runners as Mark Martin and Ricky Craven.

Nigel Kinrade

Nigel Kinrade

NASCAR Winston Cup Race 10
Save Mart Supermarkets 300
Sears Point Raceway
Sonoma, California
May 5, 1996
74 Laps, 187 Miles

RUSTY WALLACE WINS ON SEARS POINT ROAD COURSE

Terry Labonte set a new course record in qualifying on the pole, his fourth of the year, at Sears Point. At the end he had to settle for fifth behind three of NASCAR's top road racers, Rusty Wallace, Mark Martin, and Wally Dallenbach - and NAS-CAR's perennial "man to beat" - Dale Earnhardt. Wallace took over the lead from Jeff Gordon on lap 69, kept his Miller Ford out in front for the five laps needed to earn the victory, while Gordon ended up sixth. Trans-Am driver Tommy Kendall, in one of his occasional Winston Cup rides, had three laps in the lead but finished a

lap down in the MacDonald's Ford, subbing for Bill Elliott. Ricky Rudd, the second fastest qualifier, managed a seventh place finish just behind Jeff. At day's end, the three NASCAR Winston Cup leaders remained Earnhardt, 1556, Jarrett, 1441, and Labonte, 1425.

NASCAR Winston Cup Race 11
Coca-Cola 600
Charlotte Motor Speedway
Charlotte, North Carolina
May 26, 1996
400 Laps, 600 Miles

DALE JARRETT CONQUERS CHARLOTTE

Dale Jarrett convincingly demonstrated his mastery of long distance events by cruising the last 61 laps of the Coca-Cola 600, firmly in the lead, firmly in command. His victory margin over runner-up Dale

Earnhardt was a substantial 11.982 seconds. Polesitter Jeff Gordon was outsprinted for the early lead by second fastest qualifier Ricky Craven, but regained it on lap 10 and was very much in contention throughout the first half of the race. The 1995 Winston Cup titleholder finished fourth. Craven ended up an accident victim after 193 laps. Gordon's teammate, Terry Labonte qualified fourth fastest, put in a polished performance to finish third. Both Jarrett and Earnhardt came from far back qualifying positions, 15th and 20th, respectively. Bobby Labonte had a great race going, taking the lead on three occasions, the last time on lap 277, but finished far down the ladder in 22nd position. The second half of the race was owned by the two Dales, with Jarrett in charge when it counted. At day's end, the Winston Cup points leader board included Charlotte's top four with Earnhardt chalking up 1731, Jarrett, 1626, Terry Labonte, 1595, and Gordon, 1534.

NASCAR Winston Cup Race 12
Miller 500
Dover Downs Int. Speedway
Dover, Delaware
June 2, 1996
500 Laps, 500 Miles

JEFF GORDON DOMINATES AT DOVER

Blasting away from the pole, Jeff Gordon was out in front for the first 68 laps of the Miller 500, and incredibly, for the last 128 of the 500 contested. He owned a 3.90 second cushion over runner-up teammate, Terry Labonte, the fourth quickest qualifier. Dale Earnhardt, who provided most of the opposition to Gordon, was the third finisher. Usually a model of consistency, Dale Jarrett, who led the pack three times, found the wall after 374 laps. Ernie Irvan, in the Texaco Ford, had a good day, hustling from 21st at the start to fourth at the end, twice led briefly. Second fastest qualifier, Dick Trickle, in the Healthsource Ford, was never in contention, finished 28th. John Andretti in the Kmart/Little Caesar's

Ford was the leader twice, faded to 33rd. Gordon's win, his fourth of the year, moved him into the top three in Winston Cup points with 1719, behind Earnhardt, 1901, and Labonte, 1765. Jarrett's misfortune dropped him back to fourth in the standings with 1686 points. 1995 champion Gordon appears to have regained his winning form, has the momentum to surge to the top in '96.

NASCAR Winston Cup Race 13
UAW-GM Teamwork 500
Pocono International Raceway
Pocono, Pennsylvania
June 16, 1996
200 Laps, 500 Miles

NO PAUSE AT POCONO, JEFF GORDON ROLLS ON

Jeff Gordon did it again in the UAW-GM Teamwork 500, won from the pole for the second race in a row. This time he set a new track

record in qualifying, an impressive 169.175 mph. Equally impressive was his conduct during the race. Though he allowed third fastest qualifier Hut Stricklin to outjump him into the lead, and battled with Ricky Rudd for early honors, Gordon beat back a series of challenges once he got in front on lap 56. Terry Labonte, Ricky Craven, Mark Martin, Rusty Wallace, Morgan Shepherd, Bobby Hamilton, Kyle Petty, and Geoff Bodine all had turns in the lead but Gordon prevailed. At the end, he had a comfortable 3.688 second margin over Rudd, the runner-up, with Geoff Bodine the third place finisher. Bodine's performance was noteworthy, coming as it did, from 26th place at the start. Dale Jarrett had a second unhappy outing in a row, retiring early with mechanical problems. Ernie Irvan, Brett Bodine, and Bobby Labonte were sidelined early by accidents. Gordon's campaign to repeat his '95 Winston Cup title now appears to be in top gear. The top four Winston Cup points earners were Dale Earnhardt, 1968, Terry Labonte, 1916, Jeff Gordon, 1904, and Dale Jarrett, 1735.

Steve Swope

Steve Swope

NASCAR Winston Cup Race 14
Miller 400
Michigan International Speedway
Brooklyn, Michigan
June 23, 1996
200 Laps, 400 Miles

RUSTY WALLACE SETS A NEW RACE RECORD AT MICHIGAN

Bobby Hamilton put the STP Pontiac on the pole but Rusty Wallace put his Miller Ford into victory circle in the Miller 400, setting a new race record in the process with a 166.033 mph average speed. Wallace, coming up steadily from an 18th starting position, led only once, the last ten laps, including the all-important final circuit. Jeff Gordon threatened to make it three victories in a row, leading three times, the last time on lap 190 of the 200 contested, but ended up in sixth place. Terry Labonte and Sterling Marlin sparred regularly throughout the contest with runner-up Labonte having the edge over third place Marlin at the end. Jimmy Spencer, in the Camel Ford, had a good outing, gaining 36 places from his 40th starting slot to finish fourth. Polesitter Hamilton sprinted off into the lead for the first five laps but faded out of serious contention. Wallace now has three wins for the season, second only to Gordon with five, while Earnhardt and Labonte weigh in with two each. The Winston Cup ladder remained unchanged at the top; Earnhardt, ninth today, with 2106, Labonte with 2091, and Gordon with 2059.

NASCAR Winston Cup Race 15
Pepsi 400
Daytona International Speedway
Daytona Beach, Florida
July 6, 1996
160 Laps, 400 Miles

MARLIN MASTERS DAYTONA AGAIN

Sterling Marlin, in the Kodak Chevrolet, outjumped polesitter Jeff Gordon at the start of the Pepsi 400 and outgunned him and the rest of the Pepsi 400 field at the checker. Marlin led the last 30 laps but had only a thin .104 of a second margin over a fast closing Terry Labonte, in the Kellogg's Chevrolet, at the end. DuPont standard bearer Gordon salvaged third place and Dale Earnhardt, in the GM Goodwrench Chevrolet, grabbed fourth, good enough to maintain his Winston Cup lead over Labonte by a slim margin; 2266 to Labonte's 2261. Gordon retained third place in the standings at 2229 over Dale Jarrett, today's sixth place finisher, with 2029. Marlin's crew again provided the pit stop strategy necessary to prevail in long, superspeedway races. The race was remarkably accident free with only Kenny Wallace and Greg Sacks sidelined prematurely. Sterling Marlin's win elevated him to the select company of multiple race winners in '96, and secured fifth place in the Winston Cup standings behind Jarrett.

NASCAR Winston Cup Race 16
Jiffy Lube 300
New Hampshire Int. Speedway
Loudon, New Hampshire
July 14, 1996
300 Laps, 317.4 Miles

ERNIE IRVAN NAILS DOWN NEW HAMPSHIRE WIN

Ernie Irvan, aboard the Texaco Ford, had been a pole winner, a front runner, and a race leader on occasions all year. This time he made it stick, running out the last 12 laps of the Jiffy Lube 300 in front, after three other tours in the lead. He had a comfortable 5.470 second cushion over teammate Dale Jarrett in the Quality Care Ford at the checker. Ricky Rudd and Jeff Burton completed a Ford sweep of the top four finishing slots. Polesitter Ricky Craven led only the first lap, giving way to Bobby Hamilton's STP Pontiac, the other occupant of the front starting row. Irvan first took the lead on lap 57, the first of his four tours out front, was never out of contention.

Dale Earnhardt's atypical 12th place finish cost him the Winston Cup point lead, his 2398 points being edged by Labonte's 2416. Jeff Gordon retired after 253 laps with ignition problems, but held on to third place in the points chase with 2300. At the halfway mark in the season, the rest of the top ten were Jarrett, 2204, Marlin, 2054, Rudd, 2033, Schrader, 2013, Musgrave, 1934, Wallace, 1933, and Martin, 1874.

NASCAR Winston Cup Race 17
Miller 500
Pocono International Raceway
Pocono, Pennsylvania
July 21, 1996
200 Laps, 500 Miles

RUSTY WALLACE WINS POCONO'S MILLER 400

Synergy is a major item in corporate deal making. For Rusty Wallace, it's also a major item in race winning. If the race has Miller in the title, Wallace, in his Miller Ford, is likely to be an extra tough competitor. The Miller 400 at Pocono was the latest to fall into this pattern. Starting back in the 13th slot, Wallace kept his right foot down all the way, finally poked the Miller Ford's nose in front on lap 171 of the 200 contested. He was never headed, though runner-up, Ricky Rudd, in the Tide Ford, made it close. Only .300 of a second separated them at the end. Quality Care Ford driver Dale Jarrett, in another fine example of well planned superspeedway strategy, took third place, followed by teammate Ernie Irvan in the Texaco Ford. Polesitter Mark Martin, in the Valvoline Ford, led the first 36 laps, managed ninth place at the end. Points leader Terry Labonte, in the Kellogg's Chevrolet, checked in in 16th place for a 2531 Winston Cup points total. Second place points man Dale Earnhardt finished only two places higher at 14th for a total of 2519. Jeff Gordon's seventh place helped him retain third place in the standings at 2451.

Nigel Kinrade

NASCAR Winston Cup Race 18
Diehard 500
Talladega Superspeedway
Talladega, Alabama
July 28, 1996
188 Laps, 500 Miles

JEFF GORDON TAKES TALLADEGA'S SHORTENED DIEHARD 500, TOPS THE WINSTON CUP CHARTS

Jeff Gordon loves big money races. He should. The 1995 champion took home more than a quarter million dollars ($272,500) at Talladega's Diehard 500. Moreover, he only had to run 129 laps, instead of the scheduled 188 to collect the bulging purse. A huge crowd faithfully waited out a rain delay of almost four hours. Gordon's chief competitor, Dale Earnhardt, got the opposite side of the coin. He survived a terrifying accident on lap 118 which involved 11 cars including the Chevrolet of Gordon teammate Terry Labonte, the Winston Cup points leader going into today's event. Earnhardt fractured one collar bone and his sternum, was detained in a nearby Birmingham hospital overnight. Labonte was physically unhurt, but suffered in the points area, as did Earnhardt. The accident caused the race to be delayed by 15 minutes, and the field was notified that when it resumed, there would be only five more laps under green. On the restart, Gordon led, followed by Jimmy Spencer, Dale Jarrett, Rusty Wallace, and Kyle Petty. Jarrett got a great start, passed Spencer *and* Gordon to lead the first two laps under green. He couldn't make it stick, however. Gordon repassed with three laps to go to take the victory. Spencer faded to fifth at the end, Wallace to tenth, and Petty to twelfth.

Mark Martin and Ernie Irvan came on strong to nail down the third and fourth slots. Irvan and Sterling Marlin, running behind Earnhardt, triggered the huge crash, which saw Earnhardt's Chevrolet turned almost directly into the wall. Earnhardt's car was then hit head on by at least two of the drivers behind the original contact, who couldn't avoid the tangle. Gordon admitted that he was lucky to be in the right place at the right time and gave Ward Burton credit for an assist. $160,000 of his big payday was in the form of an R.J. Reynolds bonus for winning while atop the Winston Cup points. For Earnhardt, the big question was could he even start the big Brickyard 400 the following Saturday to protect any further deterioration in his point position? Mike Skinner would be standing by to offer any help required. Today's surprise polesitter, Jeremy Mayfied, finished 16th in the RCA Ford.

The leaders in Winston Cup points following the Talladega event were Gordon with 2631, Terry Labonte with 2622, an unlucky but resilient Earnhardt with 2608, and Jarrett with 2549.

Brickyard 400
Indianapolis Motor Speedway
Indianapolis, Indiana
August 3, 1996
160 Laps, 400 Miles

BRICKYARD 400 FALLS TO DALE JARRETT

Dale Jarrett and his Ford Quality Care/Ford Credit Thunderbird made it a sweep of Winston Cup's three biggest races, adding the Brickyard 400 laurels to his wins in the Daytona 500 and the Coca-Cola 600. Jarrett's chief opposition was teammate Ernie Irvan who finished a scant .0936 of a second behind in the Texaco Ford. Jarrett walked away not only with the year's long distance honors but $564,035 of the $4.8 million purse. Jeff Gordon set a record in taking the pole, 176.417 mph, but fell victim to a cut tire induced crash after only 40 laps. This misfortune bounced him out of the Winston Cup points lead, down to fourth place in the standings with 2688. Terry Labonte, the third place finisher today, rose to the top of the points chase with 2792. A courageous Dale Earnhardt, still suffering from his Talladega injuries, lasted nine laps in the GM Goodwrench Chevrolet, before handing it over to Mike Skinner. His discomfort was rewarded with a 15th place finish and second in the points standings at 2731. Winner Jarrett moved up to third place on the ladder with 2729 points on the basis of his victory. Sensational rookie Johnny Benson and Irvan swapped the lead several times in the middle segment of the race. Benson ended up eighth. Irvan's victory chances were hampered by a cut tire in the late stages of the event. Kyle Petty also cut a tire and crashed taking a disappointed Sterling Marlin with him. The last two laps were run under caution but Jarrett had things pretty well wrapped up anyway.

Nigel Kinrade

NASCAR Winston Cup Race 20
The Bud at the Glen
Watkins Glen International
Watkins Glen, New York
August 11, 1996
90 Laps, 220.5 Miles

GEOFF BODINE
BEATS THE ODDS,
WINS AT WATKINS GLEN

Winless in his previous 53 Winston Cup outings, Geoff Bodine gambled at the Glen, and won the Budweiser-backed race. In his first outing under QVC colors, Bodine's bet that he could complete the 220 miles around the beautiful road course with only two pit stops for fuel, instead of the standard three, paid off. At the end he was .440 of a second ahead of Terry Labonte, who took over the lead from polesitter Dale Earnhardt on lap 30 of the 90 contested. Earnhardt put another jewel in his "Iron Man" crown by going the entire distance in pain and finishing sixth without the readily available assistance of standby driver David Green. Earnhardt did, however, use Green's seat in his Chevrolet. Mark Martin, one of NASCAR's premier road course chauffeurs, took down third place. Jeff Gordon, in the thick of a four-way fight to retain his Winston Cup title, was fourth. Bodine was lucky to catch a caution flag attributable to Ricky Craven's lost engine for his first pit stop on lap 63. A slight slip by Ken Schrader, leading on lap 82, gave Bodine the opening to get in front, where he stayed for the eight laps remaining. For Bodine, the victory was a happy respite from a siege of problems associated with starting his own team. Labonte, 2967, Earnhardt, 2899, Gordon, 2848, and Jarrett, 2820, remained atop the Winston Cup standings. Jarrett qualified second fastest but finished a disappointing 24th.

Nigel Kinrade

NASCAR Winston Cup Race 21
GM Goodwrench Dealer 400
Michigan International Speedway
Brooklyn, Michigan
August 18, 1996
200 Laps, 400 Miles

DALE JARRETT TAKES THE HIGH LINE TO MICHIGAN VICTORY

Passing the race leader on the high side of Michigan International Speedway's ultra fast banks is a daunting exercise. Dale Jarrett took the plunge in his Quality Care Ford Credit Thunderbird and picked up the winner's chips. Valvoline driver Mark Martin, also Ford mounted, was the loser, had to settle for second place. Martin had led the previous 87 laps until Jarrett's daring lap 193 maneuver. Jeff Burton won the pole, but was outgunned at the start by Dick Trickle, who gave way to Bobby Labonte, the second fastest qualifier. Of this trio, only Jeff Burton made the top ten at the finish. Third place went to Terry Labonte, followed by Ernie Irvan and Jeff Gordon. Dale

Earnhardt managed to catch a late race spin, stayed off the wall, and finished 17th. The day's proceedings produced a shuffle in the Winston Cup point standings with Terry Labonte on top at 3137 points. Jeff Gordon and Dale Earnhardt tied for second with 3003 and Dale Jarrett fourth with 3000. Clearly, the four driver contest for the '96 Winston Cup was too close to call at this stage.

NASCAR Winston Cup Race 22
Goody's Headache Powder 500
Bristol Motor Speedway
Bristol, Tennessee
August 24, 1996
500 Laps, 266.5 Miles

RUSTY WALLACE WALTZES TO TOP HONORS AT BRISTOL

From the time Rusty Wallace first poked the nose of his Miller Ford in front for the first time on lap 100, the Goody's 500, under Bristol's

lights, was under his control. Wallace stayed out in the lead for 70 laps on this tour and completed the last 160 laps in the same winning fashion. In between, he led on two other occasions posting 77 laps and 45 laps out front on his second and third tours in the lead. Only second fastest qualifier Jeff Gordon had a shot at the flying Wallace and his bid fell short by .630 of a second. Polesitter Mark Martin, in the Valvoline Ford, lasted only nine laps in the lead giving way to Gordon but stayed with the front runners to finish third. Terry Labonte qualified his Kellogg's Chevrolet in the third slot, ended up fifth, good enough to maintain his Winston Cup points lead at 3292, Gordon checked in with 3178 points and Dale Jarrett, today's fourth place finisher, gained third place in the points chase with 3165. Dale Earnhardt could improve his 24th qualifying position by only one place but held onto fourth position in the Winston Cup points with 3094. A bump from Lake Speed put him into the wall and acounted for his poor showing.

Nigel Kinrade

NASCAR Winston Cup Race 23
Mountain Dew Southern 500
Darlington Raceway
Darlington, South Carolina
September 1, 1996
367 Laps, 500 Miles

DARLINGTON DUEL GOES TO JEFF GORDON

Fiercely contested until the final countdown, the Mountain Dew Southern 500 went to Jeff Gordon, in the DuPont Chevrolet, over a tenacious Hut Stricklin, in the Circuit City Ford. Although the lead changed hands 29 times over the 500 mile contest and 14 drivers had at least one lap in front, the contest came down to Gordon and Stricklin. In the end, Gordon just had too much firepower for Stricklin and cruised to the checker with a comfortable 5.230 second cushion. Stricklin did salvage second place. Mark Martin had his second good outing in a row, again finishing third. Ken Schrader, in the Budweiser Chevrolet, finished fourth, after starting in the same slot. Dale

Jarrett, the polesitter, had a chance at a $1 million Winston bonus but was shuffled down to 14th at the finish. Terry Labonte, the Winston Cup points leaders, could do no better than 26th today, but his 3382 points total kept him on the top rung of the ladder, followed by Gordon with 3358 and Jarrett, 3291. Dale Earnhardt came home in 12th place, just where he started, still solidly in the fourth slot in the points chase with 3221.

NASCAR Winston Cup Race 24
Miller 400
Richmond International Raceway
Richmond, Virginia
September 7, 1996
400 Laps, 400 Miles

ERNIE IRVAN OUTGUNS JEFF GORDON AT RICHMOND

Ernie Irvan bested Jeff Gordon in a crowd pleasing late race duel in Richmond's Miller 400. It was close.

Only .10 of a second separated Irvan's Texaco Ford and Gordon's DuPont Chevrolet at the checker. Irvan came from a far back 16th starting position to grab the lead for the first time on lap 135 of the 400 scheduled, got it back from Gordon on lap 301. Johnny Benson then took over for 12 laps but faded to tenth. In the race's mid-section, Gordon had traded the point position with Jeff Burton and Bill Elliott. Burton stayed in contention til the end, finishing third in his Exide Batteries Ford, Elliott faded to 16th, a lap down. Dale Jarrett and Terry Labonte, in the thick of the Winston Cup title battle, finished third and fourth today, but Labonte remained on top at this stage with 3542, a paper thin margin over Gordon at 3538. Jarrett's third place total of 3456 afforded him a bigger cushion over Dale Earnhardt, 3324, who had another disappointing 20th place today. Quick-thinking Irvan not only had to beat Gordon but an engine that cut out in the course of the race. Flipping a switch to the back up ignition system saved the day.

NASCAR Winston Cup Race 25
MBNA 500
Dover Downs Int. Speedway
Dover, Delaware
September 15, 1996
500 Laps, 500 Miles

JEFF GORDON GRABS MBNA 500 AT DOVER

Jeff Gordon, winner of his last two outings at Dover, was clearly the man to beat in the MBNA 500. No other driver was quite up to the task today. Second finisher Rusty Wallace, who never led a lap, was the closest at the end, .441 of a second behind. Most of Gordon's opposition came from Dale Jarrett who traded the lead with the '95 Winston Cup Champion three times in the closing stages. Jarrett ended up third. Bobby Labonte had a good day, putting the Interstate Batteries Ford on the pole and finishing fourth. 91 of the 500 laps were run under caution flags which flew on 14 separate occasions. Among the ten accident victims was Ernie Irvan, a winner his last time out. Gordon's eighth win of the season, in the DuPont Chevrolet, vaulted him to the top of the Winston Cup standings with 3723 points over Terry Labonte whose 21st finishing position earned him a total of 3647. Jarrett occupied third place in the season's standings with 3626, while fourth remained in the possession of Dale Earnhardt, 3444, who managed only a lackluster, for him, 16th place today.

Nigel Kinrade

NASCAR Winston Cup Race 26
Hanes 500
Martinsville Speedway
Martinsville, Virginia
September 21, 1996
500 Laps, 500 Miles

GORDON MAKES IT TWO IN A ROW AT MARTINSVILLE

Martinsville's Hanes 500 fell to a surging Jeff Gordon who made it two in a row in his DuPont Chevrolet. Polesitter Bobby Hamilton, in the STP Pontiac, fought Gordon on even terms right up to the end, when he was pipped for runner-up honors by Terry Labonte in a last lap restart. Second fastest qualifier Rusty Wallace sprinted into the lead at the start, held on for 35 laps before giving way to Hamilton. This set the stage for the Gordon-Hamilton battle, settled in Gordon's favor. Labonte led for a single lap, 388, and only these four were ever out front at any stage. The race was remarkably accident-free with Sterling Marlin the only victim. Gordon's back-to-back victories padded his Winston Cup points lead. At day's end, the top three were Gordon, 3902, Labonte, 3822, and Jarrett, 3741. Dale Earnhardt came home in 15th place today but retained the fourth slot in the standings at 3562 points. John Andretti was in third place for the last lap shoot-out, maintained that Hamilton bumped him into his fifth place finish, behind Rick Mast, the fourth place finisher.

Nigel Kinrade

Jeff Burton had a good day, moving up to fourth place from 14th on the starting grid. When the Winston Cup points were posted, Gordon had 4088, Labonte, 3977, Jarrett, 3906, and Earnhardt, 3737. For the fans at one of NASCAR's pioneer tracks it was a sad day. No Winston Cup events are scheduled for '97 at North Wilkesboro.

NASCAR Winston Cup Race 28
UAW-GM Quality 500
Charlotte Motor Speedway
Charlotte, North Carolina
October 6, 1996
500 Miles, 334 Laps

TERRY LABONTE BREAKS GORDON'S WIN STREAK, TAKES CHARLOTTE VICTORY

No streak lasts forever and Jeff Gordon's came to a halt at three in the UAW-GM Quality 500 at Charlotte. Teammate and friendly rival, Terry Labonte, in the Kellogg's Chevrolet, stepped in to annex top honors and his second win of the year. Gordon led the first six laps from his second starting position, was never again a factor due to an off-song motor. His far down 31st finishing position left him only a single point ahead of Labonte in the Winston Cup standings, despite his ten wins to Labonte's two. Mark Martin earned runner-up honors but could put no pressure on Labonte who enjoyed a comfortable 3.84 second margin at the checker. Consistent Dale Jarrett chalked up another solid third place. Sterling Marlin gave the Kodak Chevrolet a strong ride, hustling up to fourth place from 33rd on the starting grid. Polesitter Bobby Labonte was a strong contender in the first half of the event before being sidelined with engine failure. The points leaders at race end were Gordon, 4163, Labonte, 4162, Jarrett, 4071, and Dale Earnhardt, today's sixth place finisher, 3892. Gordon's slim margin brought the last three Winston Cup races; Rockingham, Phoenix, and Atlanta into sharp focus.

NASCAR Winston Cup Race 27
Tyson Holly Farms 400
North Wilkesboro Speedway
North Wilkesboro, No. Carolina
September 29, 1996
400 Laps, 250 Miles

JEFF GORDON ROLLS TO THIRD STRAIGHT VICTORY AT NORTH WILKESBORO

Jeff Gordon made it three wins in a row in the Tyson Holly Farms 400 at North Wilkesboro. His tenth victory of the year in the 27 events contested gave him an incredible .370 "batting" average and a 111 point cushion over Terry Labonte in the Winston Cup standings. Equally incredible is his four wins in the last five races. Labonte finished fifth today. A resurgent Dale Earnhardt provided most of Gordon's opposition, but was 1.73 seconds behind, in second place, at the finish. Dale Jarrett overcame a lowly 30th place start to finish third. Ted Musgrave captured the pole position but finished two laps down in 19th place.

NASCAR Winston Cup Race 29
AC-Delco 400
North Carolina Motor Speedway
Rockingham, North Carolina
October 20, 1996
393 Laps, 400 Miles

RICKY RUDD ROLLS TO VICTORY AT ROCKINGHAM

Ricky Rudd has won at least one Winston Cup race every year since 1983. His lack of luck in the first 28 races of 1996 led many observers, and perhaps Rudd himself, to believe that his streak was doomed. Rudd, however, dispelled all the doubts with a front row qualifying spot and the victor's honors at the end. Outgunned by polesitter Dale Jarrett at the start, Rudd nosed his Tide Ford in front on lap 11 and was never out of contention. His last tour in front comprised 73 laps, and brought him the checker with a husky 3.397 second margin over Jarrett. Terry Labonte's strong third place finish earned him the Winston Cup points lead at 4327. Jeff Gordon

qualified well in the third slot, led for a single lap, 81, and faded to the 12th finishing position with handling problems. His Winston Cup points total was 4295. Jarrett checked in with 4251, and Earnhardt, ninth today, 4015.

NASCAR Winston Cup Race 30
Dura-Lube 500
Phoenix International Raceway
Phoenix, Arizona
October 27, 1996
312 Laps, 312 Miles

BOBBY HAMILTON WINS ONE FOR PETTY AND STP

Bobby Hamilton, the most successful driver of Richard Petty's famed no. 43 STP Pontiac since Petty himself, had been on the pole, in the race lead, and in late race contention at various times during the '96 season. This time he made it all the way to the winner's circle, to the immense relief of Petty and his loyal sponsors

at STP. It was Hamilton's first ever Winston Cup victory and Pontiac's first of '96. Hamilton led five times, including his final 29 lap tour in front. Points leader Terry Labonte was the key player in a separate drama. He crashed hard in a Friday practice session, broke a bone in his left hand, while totalling his primary car. While his back up car was being prepared, rival Dale Jarrett had a special steering wheel, one that he'd used in a similar situation, flown down from his shop. Labonte qualified way back in the 30th slot but worked his way up to third place at the end, just behind runner-up Mark Martin. That was two places better than fifth place finisher Jeff Gordon could do, so that Labonte goes onto the Atlanta finale with 4497 points to Gordon's 4450. He needs only an eighth place finish at Atlanta to nail down the Winston Cup title. Jarrett, today's eighth finisher, remains in the third slot with 4398 points. Dale Earnhardt, 12th today, retains fourth place with 4162. Brother Bobby Labonte earned his third pole of the year, finished ninth.

Nigel Kinrade

NASCAR Winston Cup Race 31
NAPA 500
Atlanta Motor Speedway
Atlanta, Georgia
November 10, 1996
328 Laps, 500 Miles

BIG DAY FOR THE LABONTE BROTHERS AT ATLANTA

**BOBBY NABS THE NAPA 500
TERRY TAKES THE WINSTON CUP**

Bobby Labonte made this pole position, his fourth of the year, pay off. He stayed in the lead or with the front runners all day, posting a .41 of a second margin of victory over Dale Jarrett. Jeff Gordon, the second fastest qualifier, finished third, but had to concede his '95 Winston Cup title to teammate Terry Labonte, who finished fifth, after leading on two occasions. Labonte was comfortably within the eighth place finish window he needed to clinch the '96 championship. Dale Earnhardt took down fourth place today. The Labonte brothers' father, Bob, was at the head of a major post-race family celebration. Terry's championship was his second, the first coming over a decade ago in 1984. When the shouting died down, the season ending point standings were: Terry Labonte, 4657, Jeff Gordon, 4620, Dale Jarrett, 4568, Dale Earnhardt, 4327, Mark Martin, 4278, Ricky Rudd, 3845, Rusty Wallace, 3717, Sterling Marlin, 3682, Bobby Hamilton, 3639, and Ernie Irvan, 3632. After a grueling 31 race campaign, the Hendrick Racing Team had won its second Winston Cup in a row, and finished 1-2 in the points standings, a rarity not likely to be matched anytime soon.

NASCAR Craftsman Truck Series Goes to Earnhardt Driver Ron Hornaday Jr.

Nigel Kinrade

In the course of his two decades on the Winston Cup circuit (which produced seven championships), Dale Earnhardt has seen a lot of racing drivers come and go. He should be, and is, a keen judge of driving talent. His choice, as driver of wife Teresa's entry in the NASCAR Craftsman Truck Series, Ron Hornaday Jr., brought Earnhardt's NAPA Brake Parts Chevrolet home third in the series' inaugural year of 1995. Hornaday capped that performance by taking the title in '96, ahead of Jack Sprague and Mike Skinner, the '95 champion. Skinner drives the GM Goodwrench Chevrolet fielded by Earnhardt's Winston Cup team owner, Richard Childress. Sprague's truck is owned jointly by Rick Hendrick and Jeff Gordon, the owner/driver team which nailed down the '95 Winston Cup championship. These close personal relationships clearly demonstrate that NASCAR racing is indeed a family sport.

Hornaday took the title not on speed alone, but near perfect consistency. He finished every one of the 24 races on the schedule, all but one in the top ten. He was only two laps short of completing every lap run.

While Hornaday deferred to Sprague and Skinner in the win column, one of his four victories was key to the championship. At New Hampshire, he led only one lap, the last, and that one only by a few feet. His other three victories came at Portland, Louisville, and Watkins Glen. Sprague won all five races on tracks measuring a mile or more, was upended in his title campaign by an accident at Richmond.

Skinner matched the eight victories of his championship '95 year but paid dearly for engine failure and a resultant DNF at New Hampshire, where arch rival Hornaday picked up top honors. As a consolation prize, Skinner took the $6,000 Busch Pole Award with five fastest qualifying runs. Skinner was also the series' top money winner over its two year history with $1.01 million in posted awards. After the top three points producers, Dave Rezendes, in the QVC Ford scored the most victories, with three, but would finish the season in sixth place in the points standings. Mike Bliss, in the ASE Ford, was the only other multiple race winner with two. He took down fifth place in the points standings,

behind a winless Joe Ruttman, fourth man on the series ladder at season end. Rick Carelli, tenth at year end, in the RE/MAX Chevrolet, scored a single victory as did Mark Martin, on a busman's holiday from the Winston Cup wars. Butch Miller, Jimmy Hensley, and Bryan Reffner occupied seventh, eighth, and ninth place, respectively, in the '96 points standings. Hensley was the highest placed Winston Cup regular. Other Winston Cup drivers to try their hands on the circuit included Jeff Burton, Bobby Hamilton, and Darrell Waltrip. Ernie Irvan, who is a co-owner of the 1-800-Collect Ford, was another Winston Cup stalwart to make an occasional truck foray, but, also, failed to make the winner's column. Chevrolet again took the Manufacturers' Championship. Bryan Reffner out drove a record crop of 23 first year drivers, gained the $7,700 Cintas Rookie of the Year Award.

The sophomore year for NASCAR's fastest growing series listed 144 points scoring drivers and four million dollars in prize money. Look for further expansion in 1997, with new teams, new venues - and more prize money in the mix.

Nigel Kinrade

Nigel Kinrade

1 Earnhardt's Choice... **Ron Hornaday Jr.** finished every race, 23 out of 24 in the top ten, four times in victory circle. A worthy champion. (3831 NASCAR Craftsman Truck points)

2 Fast Tracker... **Jack Sprague** won five of the seven races on tracks one mile or longer, couldn't match Hornaday's all around results. (3778 NASCAR Craftsman Truck points)

Nigel Kinrade

3 Most Victories... **Mike Skinner** matched the eight victories of his '95 championship year, won five poles, came up short on consistency. (3771 NASCAR Craftsman Truck points)

Nigel Kinrade

4 Ford Flyer... **Joe Ruttman** scored no victories but ran up front all year. (3275 NASCAR Craftsman Truck points)

5 Two Time Winner... **Mike Bliss** was regularly in contention for top honors.
(3190 NASCAR Craftsman Truck points)

6 Victor in Season Opener... **Dave Rezendes** added two more for the fourth highest win total of the year.
(3179 NASCAR Craftsman Truck points)

Nigel Kinrade

7 Top Tenner... **Butch Miller** was again one of the series' elite.
(3126 NASCAR Craftsman Truck points)

Nigel Kinrade

8 Winston Cup Warrior... **Jimmy Hensley** was the top Winston Cup regular on the circuit. (3029 NASCAR Craftsman Truck points)

Nigel Kinrade

9 Rookie of the Year... **Bryan Reffner** won Cintas Rookie of the Year honors as well as three poles, second only to Skinner in pole production. (2961 NASCAR Craftsman Truck points)

Nigel Kinrade

10 Race Winner... **Rick Carelli** notched only one victory, but regularly ran up front. (2953 NASCAR Craftsman Truck points)

Nigel Kinrade

NASCAR Craftsman Truck Race 1
Florida Dodge Dealers 400
Homestead Motorsports Complex
Homestead, Florida
March 17, 1996
167 Laps, 400 Kilometers

DAVE REZENDES ROLLS AT HOMESTEAD OPENER

1995 Champion Mike Skinner, in the black GM Goodwrench Chevrolet, didn't take the pole, as he did ten times last year but quickly made clear his designs on a repeat championship. He outsprinted polesitter and Winston Cup regular Geoff Bodine, in the QVC Ford, into the first turn and held on to his advantage for the first 53 laps before giving way to Bodine. Bodine's sojourn in front was short lived. By lap 63, Skinner was back in the lead. On lap 83, Bodine had crashed out of contention in a three way tangle with Skinner and Dave Allen. Skinner, slowed as a result of the tangle, finished far down. Dave Rezendes, in the second QVC Ford, inherited the lead on lap 81, setting up a duel with two new front runners, Jack Sprague, in the Quaker State Chevrolet, and Ron Hornaday Jr., in NAPA colors. Despite some metal-to-metal contact, Rezendes won that three way contest and started off the new season

the winner and the points leader. Not bad for someone who spent more time last year twisting wrenches than twisting steering wheels.

NASCAR Craftsman Truck Race 2
Chevrolet Desert Star Classic 300
Phoenix International Raceway
Phoenix, Arizona
April 21, 1996
186 Laps, 186 Miles

JACK SPRAGUE STARS AT PHOENIX

Jack Sprague and his Quaker State Chevrolet came out second best in a late race duel in the season opener. Not this time, Sprague emerged on top. The best that '95 Champion Mike Skinner could throw at him all afternoon wasn't enough to dislodge him from the lead on his final tour in front, a lengthy 53 laps. Only these two ever led. Skinner, the polesitter, lasted only five tours in front, before giving way to Sprague. Skinner made it 29 laps on the point on his second tour in front but couldn't hold off Sprague in the final stages, was .100 of a second behind at the checker. Butch Miller, in the Raybestos Ford, picked up third place but was never in the hunt for top honors. Sprague picked up the points leadership over Hornaday Jr.

NASCAR Craftsman Truck Race 3
Craftsman 200/NW Dodge Dealers
Portland Speedway
Portland, Oregon
May 4, 1996
200 Laps, 100 Miles

RON HORNADAY JR. HUSTLES TO PORTLAND VICTORY

Rich Bickle put his Cummins Engine Dodge on the pole but never led a lap. He was eventually sidelined with mechanical bothers on lap 184. Ron Barfield led the first 34 laps in the Super 8 Motel Ford, before fading to a lap behind at the end. Mike Skinner, in the GM Goodwrench Chevrolet, then had four tours in front. After that it was all NAPA driver Ron Hornaday, in command for the final 160 laps, though only by .644 of a second at the end. Mike Bliss, in the Team ASE Ford, grabbed runner-up honors, outmuscling Skinner in the closing stages. Hornaday's win delighted Dale Earnhardt, the astute talent scout who picked him for the drive. The victory landed him in first place in the points chase ahead of Jack Sprague, today's eighth place finisher. Dave Rezendes, the inaugural race winner was an accident victim before the halfway mark.

NASCAR Craftsman Truck Race 4
Jerr-Dan/Nelson Truck 200
by NW Dodge Dealers
Evergreen Speedway
Monroe, Washington
May 11, 1996
200 Laps, 129.2 Miles

MIKE BLISS CUTS A WINNING GROOVE AT EVERGREEN

Mike Bliss, the ASE Ford driver, knows only too well the sinking feeling of being edged out in the final stages of a major race. Washington's Evergreen Speedway presented him with the opportunity to do the edging and he responded with a .392 of a second victory margin over Ron Hornaday Jr. Surprise polesitter Tobey Butler maintained the lead for the first 12 laps, at which point Bliss took over for 93 tours. Rich Bickle then enjoyed 29 tours out front before giving way to Bliss. A determined Ron Hornaday dislodged Bliss from the lead for two laps close to the end, but couldn't make it stick. Bliss repassed and took top honors. 47 year old Dan Press nosed his Class Act Chevrolet in front of Rich Bickle for the third finishing spot. Hornaday padded his points lead.

NASCAR Craftsman Truck Race 5
NAPA 200
Tucson Raceway Park
Tucson, Arizona
May 25, 1996
200 Laps, 75 Miles

BACK IN CHAMPIONSHIP FORM, MIKE SKINNER TAKES TUCSON

Mike Skinner is a true champion, too good to be kept out of the winner's circle for long. The '95 title-holder found Tucson's tight little 3/8 mile oval to his liking, shuffled Rich Bickle, the Dodge protagonist, aside in a clever move when both were overtaking lapped traffic. Bickle led the first 126 laps and felt he had the victory in hand. Chances are he did, except for picking the wrong passing lane. Even a restart with three laps to go failed to reverse his miscue. Ford mounted Bryan Reffner was the polesitter but was outgunned by Bickle on the first lap. A solid third place for Ron Hornaday Jr. kept him on top of the points parade, ahead of Jack Sprague, fifth today, and an upwardly mobile Skinner, who promised to be in the thick of the championship battle as the season unfolded.

NASCAR Craftsman Truck Race 6
Colorado 250 by Snap-On Tools
Colorado National Speedway
Dacono, Colorado
June 1, 1996
253 Laps, 94.875 Miles

MIKE SKINNER MAKES IT TWO IN A ROW AT COLORADO

Another tight 3/8 mile oval meant another big payday for Mike Skinner. At Colorado he let polesitter Rich Bickle, in the Cummins Dodge, and Ron Hornaday Jr., in the NAPA Brake Parts Chevrolet, swap the lead twice over the first 33 laps, took over on lap 34 and was never headed for the remaining 219. Bickle gave up with engine failure before the half way mark and Hornaday slipped to eighth place at the finish. Butch Miller, in the Raybestos Ford, closed fast for second place, down .769 seconds at the checker. Winston Cup regular Jimmy Hensley, in a second Dodge, finished third. Hornaday still led the points chase but 1995 champion Mike Skinner was clearly gaining momentum in a three way championship battle with Ron Hornaday Jr. and Jack Sprague, the third contender.

Nigel Kinrade

Nigel Kinrade

NASCAR Craftsman Truck Race 7
Lund Look 225
Heartland Park Topeka
Topeka, Kansas
June 9, 1996
77 Laps, 225 Kilometers

THREE IN A ROW FOR MIKE SKINNER IN TOPEKA

At Topeka's Heartland Park road circuit, Mike Skinner, in the GM Goodwrench Chevrolet, proved that his expertise is not limited to bullrings on which he posted his two previous victories. It took him eight laps to get around polesitter Ron Hornaday Jr., in the NAPA Brake Parts Chevrolet, and he reeled off the remaining 69 laps of the Lund Look 225 in commanding fashion. Nobody else came close. Hornaday was pipped for second place by Jack Sprague, in the Quaker State Chevrolet, up from a 12th place starting position. Hornaday retained his points lead with 1142 over Skinner with 1133, but his margin was down to the single digit level. Sprague is nipping at their heels.

NASCAR Craftsman Truck Race 8
Coca-Cola 200
Bristol Motor Speedway
Bristol, Tennessee
June 22, 1996
200 Laps, 106.6. Miles

CARELLI ENDS SKINNER'S WIN STREAK AT BRISTOL

Mike Skinner's three race win streak was unceremoniously halted by a charging Rick Carelli, in the RE/MAX Ford, on Bristol's half mile oval. For more than half the race, 125 of the 200 laps scheduled, polesitter Skinner was out in front and looking like a winner. Joe Ruttman, in the Roush Performance Products Ford, shouldered him aside on lap 126, and was, in turn, displaced by Carelli, who motored to a .291 of a second margin of victory over Dave Rezendes, winner of the season opener, with Jay Sauter, in the SABCO Chevrolet, notching third place. Skinner salvaged fourth place but elbowed Ron Hornaday Jr., today's eighth place finisher, out of the top spot in points.

NASCAR Craftsman Truck Race 9
DeVilbiss Superfinish 200
Nazareth Speedway
Nazareth, Pennsylvania
June 30, 1996
152 Laps, 152 Miles

JACK SPRAGUE GETS THE NOD AT NAZARETH

Rain delayed the start of the DeVilbiss 200, which started and ended under caution. Second fastest qualifier Jack Sprague, in the Quaker State Chevrolet, was in the right place, out front, when the checkered flag waved. Jimmy Hensley put the Mopar Dodge on the pole and led the first 103 laps. Ron Hornaday Jr. then enjoyed seven laps in front. Hornaday lost out to eventual winner Sprague. Jimmy Hensley collected another Dodge powered strong second place, with Butch Miller third. Sprague's win tied Hornaday in the points chase. His two victories to Hornaday's single win made him the official leader in the points chase at this stage. Skinner's 14th place finish shuffled him back to third.

NASCAR Craftsman Truck Race 10
Sears Auto Center 200
The Milwaukee Mile
West Allis, Wisconsin
July 6, 1996
200 Laps, 200 Miles

JACK SPRAGUE MASTERS MILWAUKEE MILE

Mike Bliss set a new record in qualifying on the pole at Milwaukee, but Jack Sprague set a new race record and took down top honors in the Sears Auto Center 200. Sprague, in the Quaker State Chevrolet, was a comfortable 3.015 seconds ahead of Bill Sedgwick, in the Sears Diehard Chevrolet, at the finish, with Ron Hornaday Jr. a close third. Polesitter Bliss, in the ASE Ford, led only the first two laps, before being muscled aside by Mike Skinner, who swapped the lead regularly with eventual winner Sprague over the remaining 198 laps. Skinner slipped to seventh at the checker with Ron Hornaday Jr. taking third place. Sprague's third win made him the undisputed points leader.

NASCAR Craftsman Truck Race 11
Ford Dealers 225
Louisville Motor Speedway
Louisville, Kentucky
July 20, 1996
225 Laps, 98.4375 Miles

RON HORNADAY JR. ON TOP IN LOUISVILLE

Ford driver Ron Hornaday Jr. made his second win of the season a convincing one, leading the entire second half of the Ford Dealers 225 at Louisville. Mike Bliss, the polesitter, led the first 44 laps, twice swapped the lead with Hornaday but fell back to 13th at the end. These two were the only drivers to lead a lap. Second finisher Mike Skinner came from back in the sixth row at the start, was .661 of a second behind at the finish. Mopar Performance Dodge driver Jimmy Hensley, the Winston Cup star, finished third. Hornaday regained the points lead over Sprague and Skinner but their three way tug-of-war continued at high pitch going into the Western Auto 200.

NASCAR Craftsman Truck Race 12
Western Auto 200
I-70 Speedway
Odessa, Missouri
July 27, 1996
200 Laps, 108.6 Miles

MIKE BLISS ON TOP IN ODESSA

Mike Bliss joined the elite club of multiple race winners in the NASCAR Craftsman Truck Series with a convincing victory in the Western Auto 200 at I-70 Speedway. He and Ron Hornaday Jr. swapped the lead six times, with Bliss prevailing and Hornaday shuffled back to fourth place at the end. Mike Skinner, in the GM Goodwrench Chevrolet, and Rick Carelli, in the RE/MAX Chevrolet, notched the second and third finishing slots. Bliss sported a comfortable 1.862 second cushion over Skinner at the finish. Occupants of the top rungs of the points ladder were unchanged by today's results, Ron Hornaday, 1944, Mike Skinner, 1900, and Jack Sprague ,1882, in that order.

Nigel Kinrade

Nigel Kinrade

NASCAR Craftsman Truck Race 13	NASCAR Craftsman Truck Race 14	NASCAR Craftsman Truck Race 15
The Cummins 200	Stevens Beil/Genuine Car Parts 200	Parts America 150
Indianapolis Raceway Park	Flemington Speedway	Watkins Glen International
Indianapolis, Indiana	Flemington, New Jersey	Watkins Glen, New York
August 1, 1996	August 10, 1996	August 25, 1996
200 Laps, 137.2 Miles	204 Laps, 127.5 Miles	61 Laps, 149.45 Miles

MIKE SKINNER SWEEPS ALL 200 LAPS AT IRP

A virtuoso performance by Mike Skinner, in the GM Goodwrench Chevrolet, at Indianapolis Raceway Park saw him capture the pole for the Cummins 200 and lead every lap to victory circle. Jack Sprague, in the Quaker State Chevrolet, came closest, .741 of a second behind at the finish. He was followed by Mike Bliss, in the ASE Ford, the third place finisher. Ron Hornaday Jr., in the NAPA Brake Parts Chevrolet, took down fourth place, saw his points lead over Skinner dwindle. Hornaday led with 2104 points over Skinner with 2080 points. Skinner, the 1995 NASCAR Craftsman Truck Champion became the series' first four time winner of 1996.

MIKE SKINNER FLIES TO FLEMINGTON VICTORY

On a roll to retain his championship, Mike Skinner made it two in a row, five for the season with his Flemington victory. Rookie Bryan Reffner, won the pole, his second of the year. He led only three laps, before losing out to Skinner, ended up in 12th place. Joe Ruttman threatened Skinner with a 12 lap sojourn in front, fell out just past the halfway mark with radiator problems. Mike Bliss provided the main opposition to the winner, annexed second place, .453 of a second astern of Skinner at the end. Ron Hornaday Jr.'s sixth place today cost him the points lead which went to Skinner. Fifth place finisher Jack Sprague remained in third place in the points totals.

WATKINS GLEN GOES TO RON HORNADAY JR.

Watkins Glen's long, fast road course can pose a stiff challenge to the drivers of racing trucks. Not, however, to Ron Hornaday Jr. who led the last two thirds of the Parts America 150 there, finishing first with a handy 1.639 second advantage over Joe Nemechek, the polesitter. Nemechek, in the BellSouth Mobility Chevrolet, did not lead a lap. Mike Skinner, beside Nemechek on the front row, took over the point position for the first third of the race, ended up third. Hornaday regained his perch atop the points ladder with 2434, followed by Skinner, 2424, and by Jack Sprague, 2367, today's fourth place finisher.

NASCAR Craftsman Truck Race 16
Federated Auto Parts 250
Nashville Speedway USA
Nashville, Tennessee
August 31, 1996
255 Laps, 152 Miles

DAVE REZENDES NABS NASHVILLE VICTORY

Shut out of victory circle since the first race of the year, Dave Rezendes rebounded in Nashville's Federated Auto Parts 250, to take his second victory of '96. He had to come from a far back 14th starting position to claim the top honors. The early going was a three way battle between polesitter Jack Sprague, Ron Hornaday Jr. and Mike Skinner. Then Harry Gant had a turn in the lead, lost out to an accident. Rezendes, in the QVC Ford, was untouchable over the last 26 laps, finishing .428 of a second ahead of Hornaday, with Sprague in third place. While the three top points producers were unchanged (Hornaday, Skinner and Sprague), Rezendes solidified his hold on fourth place in the standings.

NASCAR Craftsman Truck Race 17
Fas Mart Truck Shootout
Richmond International Raceway
Richmond, Virginia
September 5, 1996
124 Laps, 91 Miles

MIKE SKINNER ROLLS TO VICTORY NO. 6 AT RAIN SHORTENED RICHMOND

Kenny Irwin Jr. was the surprise polesitter, but Mike Skinner out accelerated him into the first turn, led the first 58 laps. Winston Cup regular Mark Martin took over for 14 tours. The rest of the race belonged to Skinner. Series rival Ron Hornaday Jr. moved into second place at the end, just edging out Martin. Skinner now has six wins for the year, twice as many as any other competitor, but still trails Hornaday in the point standings. The race was halted for rain after 124 laps with the field sitting on pit row. Nonetheless, Skinner was a deserving winner. Considering the conditions, the race was remarkably accident free with only rookie Charlie Cragan and sprint car star Andy Hillenburg finding the barriers.

NASCAR Craftsman Truck Race 18
Pennzoil/VIP Tripleheader
New Hampshire Int. Speedway
Loudon, New Hampshire
September 8, 1996
206 Laps, 218 Miles

RON HORNADAY JR.'S LAST LAP PASS TAKES NEW HAMPSHIRE

Even Ron Hornaday's fiercest competitors in the NASCAR Craftsman Truck Series agree, however reluctantly, that he's the king of restarts. He added to his reputation with a thrilling last lap pass of Jack Sprague at New Hampshire to win the Pennzoil/VIP event by a mere .322 of a second. The last lap was the only one Hornaday led all day, and, of course, the only one that counted. Sprague had been battling Joe Ruttman ever since lap 18 and looked to be the winner when Ruttman fell off the pace. Mike Bliss garnered third place. Polesitter Mike Skinner started strong but lasted only 82 laps. Hornaday's prowess earned him a 150 point lead over Skinner in the points chase.

Nigel Kinrade

Nigel Kinrade

NASCAR Craftsman Truck Race 19
Hanes 250
Martinsville Speedway
Martinsville, Virginia
September 21, 1996
255 Laps, 134.1 Miles

NASCAR Craftsman Truck Race 20
Lowe's Home Improvement 250
North Wilkesboro Speedway
North Wilkesboro, North Carolina
September 28, 1996
250 Laps, 156.25 Miles

NASCAR Craftsman Truck Race 21
Kragen 151
Sears Point Raceway
Sonoma, California
October 5, 1996
60 Laps, 151.2 Miles

MIKE SKINNER MASTERS MARTINSVILLE

Bobby Hamilton in Richard Petty's STP Chevrolet won the pole and got off to a great start, leading the first 116 laps. By lap 143 he was out, with steering problems. That left the fight up front to Butch Miller, in the Raybestos Ford, and Mike Skinner, in the GM Goodwrench Chevrolet. Miller prevailed in the first part of the duel but Skinner had a comfortable 1.04 second cushion at the end. Jack Sprague notched third place, up from tenth at the start. Ron Hornaday Jr.'s fourth place kept him on top of the points parade, but Skinner, with his seventh win of the year, was whittling down the margin.

MARK MARTIN TAMES NORTH WILKESBORO

Mark Martin started on the front row of the Lowe's 250 at North Wilkesboro but it took him 178 laps to get into the lead. Once in front he could not be caught and ran out the rest of the 250 laps with a .780 second edge on Jack Sprague. Polesitter Johnny Benson was out front and flying for the first 77 laps before Mike Skinner took over. Skinner was passed by Jack Sprague, who garnered the runner-up spot at the end, ahead of Butch Miller. Skinner was shuffled back into ninth place at the finish. The series points leader, Ron Hornaday Jr. had a rare bad day, ended up back in 22nd place but still atop the points chart.

DAVE REZENDES RIDES FORD TO SEARS POINT WIN

Qvc Ford driver Dave Rezendes started back in eighth position, gained the lead at the halfway mark and cruised to victory by a handsome 1.177 second margin over Ron Hornaday, in the NAPA Brake Parts Chevrolet, who started on the front row. Polesitter Mike Skinner, in the GM Goodwrench Chevrolet, swapped the lead with Hornaday seven times in the first half of the race before settling for third place at the end. With only three races left, Hornaday's 96 point lead over Skinner, while vulnerable, is a sizeable obstacle to Skinner's designs on a repeat truck championship.

NASCAR Craftsman Truck Race 22
Ford Dealers 300 by Ford Credit
Mesa Marin Raceway
Bakersfield, California
October 13, 1996
300 Laps, 150 Miles

NASCAR Craftsman Truck Race 23
GM Goodwrench/Delco Battery 200
Phoenix International Raceway
Phoenix, Arizona
October 26, 1996
180 Laps, 300 Kilometers

NASCAR Craftsman Truck Race 24
Carquest 420K
Las Vegas Motor Speedway
Las Vegas, Nevada
November 3, 1996
175 Laps, 420 Kilometers

MIKE SKINNER SCORES AT BAKERSFIELD IN LAST DITCH TITLE BATTLE

If Mike Skinner's bid for a repeat championship falls short, it won't be for lack of trying. He won the Bakersfield round handily, nearly a full second ahead of the runner-up. Only problem was that the runner-up was Ron Hornaday Jr., the polesitter and current points leader. With the season's last two events coming up at Phoenix and Las Vegas, some misfortune will have to fall to Hornaday, in the NAPA Brake Parts Chevrolet, for Skinner, in the GM Goodwrench Chevrolet, to prevail. 86 points separate the two going into Phoenix. Joe Ruttman, in the Line-X Ford, placed third today while the third driver in the points parade, Jack Sprague notched fifth with Mike Bliss in between.

JACK SPRAGUE SCORES AT PHOENIX

Polesitter Jack Sprague had stiff opposition from Pennzoil Chevrolet driver Johnny Benson, the other occupant of the front starting row, but scored his fourth win of the year at Phoenix International Raceway. This pair swapped the lead four times with Sprague up front when it counted. Joe Ruttman, in the LCI Ford, nailed down third place. Neither of the two top title contenders had a banner day but Mike Skinner's fourth place earned him a few points on leader Ron Hornaday, seventh today. With the season finale coming up in a week at the fast new Las Vegas track. Skinner trailed by 72 points. Sprague has third place in the championship locked up, could still theoretically win it all.

SPRAGUE SUPERB AT LAS VEGAS
HORNADAY THE NEW SERIES CHAMPION

Jack Sprague finished the season in glory, winning the Carquest 420K at Las Vegas' fast, beautiful 1.5 mile oval. His $80,825 payday was the year's biggest. Moreover, he nudged Mike Skinner, seventh today, out of second place in the year's points standings. The new series champion Ron Hornaday motored to the title with a conservative tenth place finish but still earned, "You done a good job" plaudits from team owner Dale Earnhardt. The race was a battle between Sprague and Ernie Irvan until Irvan dropped out on lap 140 with mechanical problems. Another Winston Cup regular, Bill Elliott, notched second place while Joe Ruttman finished third.

Nigel Kinrade

Drivers

A Changing of the Guard

By David Phillips

The PPG Indy Car World Series witnessed a changing of the guard in 1996. Honda, Firestone, and Target/Ganassi Racing came to the fore even as traditional powerhouses Penske Racing and Ilmor/Mercedes-Benz went winless.

Simultaneously, Jimmy Vasser, Alex Zanardi, Andre Ribeiro, Gil de Ferran, Adrian Fernandez, Christian Fittipaldi, and Greg Moore established themselves as front runners to carry the sport into the 21st century. Michael Andretti and Al Unser Jr. continued to reinforce their status as the established stars of today. Meanwhile, one of yesterday's legendary stars - Emerson Fittipaldi - stared the prospects of retirement squarely in the eye.

Sadly, 1996 will also be remembered as the year in which push finally came to shove in the tug of war between Championship Auto Racing Teams and the Indianapolis Motor Speedway for control of Indy car racing. Sadder still, IndyCar racing lost several friends this year including driver Jeff Krosnoff, safety marshall Gary Avrin, and the sport's guiding light - former PPG racing director Jim Chapman - who died in October after a long battle with cancer.

Yet the ebbs of 1996 should not detract from a remarkable season which saw 17 drivers reach the podium, three new race winners, and such even competition on the engine, chassis, and tire fronts that three different engine manufacturers, three different makes of chassis, and both brands of tires went to the starting line at Laguna Seca with a chance to share post-season honors with the PPG Cup Champion.

That Vasser should win the title in such a year is a tribute to Honda, Firestone, Reynard, Target/Ganassi Racing, and his own blend of skill and mental toughness.

After six years marked in equal amounts by risk taking and inconsistent results, Chip Ganassi made three major moves shortly after the conclusion of the 1995 season. First, he switched from Ford to Honda; next he switched from Goodyear to Firestone; then he hired Formula One expatriate Alex Zanardi.

But as Ganassi is quick to point out, sometimes the moves you don't make are the most important. Thus he stuck with Vasser - 1995's Most Improved Driver - and went into the season banking on two drivers who had no IndyCar wins between them. He also retained the balance of a team which had begun to jell the previous season, including managing director Tom Anderson, team manager Mike Hull, race engineers Morris Nunn and Julian Robertson, and Vasser's crew chief Grant Weaver, with veteran Robin Hill coming from Team Rahal to oversee preparations on Zanardi's car.

That stability, coupled with Honda's power and reliability, and Firestone's grip and durability, helped stake Vasser to an early lead in the PPG Cup points race. In the season opener at the new Homestead Motor Sports Complex, he out maneuvered Gil de Ferran on a late restart to score his first IndyCar victory. This came after Paul Tracy had dominated much of the race only to go out with transmission failure.

Next on the agenda was another first - the PPG Indy Car World Series' first appearance in South America at the trapezoidally configured Emerson Fittipaldi Speedway near Rio de Janeiro. Although his crew inadvertently placed a mismatched set of tires on his car at mid-race, Vasser took advantage of some late attrition to salvage a useful eighth place.

Firestone, which struggled at times on temporary circuits in 1995, produced a superior tire for the streets of Surfers Paradise. Vasser took full advantage of that edge, claiming his first IndyCar pole, then, together with Scott Pruett, the Firestone factory driver, loping away from the field. Showing increasing maturity, Vasser and the Target/Ganassi team didn't panic when he took on a short fuel

load on their second stop. They made a third stop under a timely full course yellow without missing a beat and came home first when Pruett slowed with fuel concerns of his own.

Jimmy Vasser was twice lucky at Long Beach, first surviving a wheel-banging incident with Paul Tracy, then scooping up his third win when Gil de Ferran's dominant Reynard-Honda faltered within sight of the checkered flag.

After a mediocre seventh place finish at Nazareth, Vasser set off for the inaugural U.S. 500 at Michigan International Speedway in command of the PPG Cup points race. Vasser solidified his role as the man to beat in 1996 by charging to his first superspeedway pole at 232.025 mph only to get tangled up in an embarrassing pace lap crash that damaged more than a dozen cars.

Amazingly, all but Fernandez took the restart and Vasser and his crew worked with their backup Reynard all day to get it right for the final sprint to the finish. Although outpaced at times by Zanardi, Moore, and Parker Johnstone, only Vasser and Andre Ribeiro were upfront at the finish. When Ribeiro pitted for a splash of fuel, Vasser's fourth win of the year was assured.

So, too, was his PPG Cup title, or so it seemed. In contrast to conventional wisdom that the "real" Indy car season begins after the month of May, the fact of the matter is that all five of the men who have led the PPG points race since 1991 on June 1 have gone on to win the PPG Cup itself. That would also be the case with Vasser - but not without a few anxious moments.

Through June, July, and August Vasser and his crew looked like anything but PPG Cup champions. If he wasn't off the pace at Milwaukee (where his short oval set-up was again lacking) or Detroit (where Firestone's rain tires were outclassed), Vasser or the team made costly mistakes like a spin in the rain at Portland and a failed pit strategy at Cleveland. After a rather tentative eighth place at Toronto, Vasser took the pole at the Michigan 500. He then proceeded to drop through the field like a stone once the race began, thanks to a miscommunication with the crew that saw him start the race with a set-up more suited to qualifying than 500 miles.

Yet for all their troubles, Vasser and the Target/Ganassi team were flawless in executing one aspect of their game plan: they *finished* races. Embarrassingly uncompetitive at Michigan, Vasser nevertheless took advantage of attrition to finish ninth. While other championship pretenders self-destructed (or in the cases of Michael Andretti and Al Unser Jr., suffered critical mechanical failures), Vasser reeled off finish after finish. A close second place to Zanardi at Mid-Ohio stopped the bleeding. Vasser next caught a big break at Road America when Unser blew up on the final lap as he was poised to take the PPG Cup points lead. Yet, Michael Andretti's exquisitely judged win at Vancouver moved him to within striking distance of his second PPG Cup when Vasser was penalized for a pit lane violation, after his speed governor apparently malfunctioned.

That set up a showdown at Laguna Seca, with Jimmy Vasser needing a fifth to clinch; not a major undertaking on the face of it, but anything could happen. This weekend, the breaks went Vasser's way. Andretti lost most of the opening practice session to a mechanical failure and never found the right set-up, while Unser crashed and fell behind as well. Vasser survived an off-track excursion of his own, then put in a seamless drive that had him in contention for his fifth win of the year until he blistered a tire and yielded third place to Scott Pruett on the last lap.

As Vasser himself notes, his season was a paradoxical one. "Talk about a season of ups and downs, in one way you can say it was very consistent but in another way you can say it was very inconsistent," he says. "You keep going back to the fact that we finished every race. There were four or five races in the middle where, at the time you thought 'What a useless weekend - I got three points.' And you leave thinking you got nothing. But all that added up to the difference that we had at the end. So the fact that the race car was running at the end of all the races was really the difference."

Underlining Target/Ganassi's rise to the top of the IndyCar heap is the fact that Vasser was the only driver to amass more PPG points than teammate Alex Zanardi. Championed by Reynard as a superb technical driver, Alex slotted into the no.4 Target-Reynard and immediately contributed to the team's extensive preseason test program. After a difficult debut in Homestead, where a wheel fell off his car at mid-race, he served notice that he would be a force to be reckoned with by taking the pole at Rio and leading much of the race before losing out in the end-game pit stop strategy.

He was seldom short of spectacular from there on, leading the U.S. 500 handily before an enormous engine failure for example, but couldn't buy a break until he led virtually flag-to-flag at Portland for his first win. Beaten by a whisker by de Ferran at Cleveland, he was also forced to concede to an on-form Fernandez at Toronto. He dominated at Michigan again, only to crash when the handling deteriorated, but rebounded with a resounding victory at Mid-Ohio. He kept his championship hopes alive with a rough and tumble third at Road America (where he was fined $20,000 for a bumping incident with de Ferran) only to exit the Vancouver race (and the race for the PPG Cup title) when he tangled with a tenacious P.J. Jones while leading.

Undeterred, he finished the season in spectacular fashion, taking to the dirt to pass an unsuspecting Bryan Herta on the last lap at Laguna Seca to earn his third win of the year.

Open and honest almost to a fault, Alex Zanardi's biggest asset may well be the magical chemistry he has so clearly developed with the Target/Ganassi team, in particular Chip Ganassi and Morris Nunn, his star-caliber engineer. With a season's worth of experience to his credit he ranks as an early favorite to contend for the 1997 PPG Cup. He was the clear cut winner of "Rookie of the Year" honors and the accompanying $50,000 honorarium.

In many people's eyes, Michael Andretti had his finest season as an IndyCar driver in 1996. After a problematic start to the campaign, in which he collected Mauricio Gugelmin at Homestead and Long Beach, Paul Tracy at Surfers Paradise, and Teo Fabi at Long Beach, he was placed on probation for rough driving. Worse yet, he had just two finishes - a seventh and a ninth to show for his work. What's more, the new Ford-Cosworth XD engine had yet to reach its potential.

Yet Andretti and the Newman-Haas team pulled it together at Nazareth, where he stormed to a faultless victory after Tracy bowled over several crew members on a pit stop. After an early departure in the U.S. 500, Andretti took advantage of two late yellows to pass, then held off Unser at Milwaukee for his second win. At Detroit, a week later, he upstaged teammate Christian Fittipaldi in the closing stages to score his third win in four races.

Mechanical problems dogged Andretti through the balance of June and July, but he clawed his way home to third at Mid-Ohio then took advantage of Unser's wretched luck at Road America to bring the Kmart/Texaco-Havoline Lola its fourth win of the year. Two weeks later he picked his way through the wreckage of Zanardi's run-in with Jones to score his fifth win of the season and headed to Laguna Seca in a buoyant frame of mind. But a differential failure in the first practice session put him behind the eight ball and he never recovered, eventually passing a cooperative Fittipaldi on the final lap to draw level with winner Zanardi on points. He placed runner-up in the championship on the basis of his five victories, the most of any driver.

Al Unser Jr. was as impressive as ever despite his first winless season since 1987. That he failed to mount the top step of the podium was scant reward for a season that should have produced at least two wins and further underlined the depth of his fierce determination and well-honed talent.

Milwaukee and Road America stand out as the high/low points of the season. Unser waged a classic battle with Andretti on the Milwaukee Mile, one which saw Andretti take advantage of his soft, option compound Goodyears to lead early in each segment, only to fade as Unser's harder primaries came into their own. Unser was on his way to victory when a late full course yellow erased his margin over Andretti, the more so because of IndyCar's new restart procedure that shuffled lapped cars to the back of the pack, giving the contenders a clean run at the leader.

His tires not up to peak operating temperature after several laps under yellow, Unser was a sitting duck for Andretti. Then, just as Unser's tires started coming around, another fulll course yellow recycled the situation, giving the Newman-Haas Lola's softer Goodyears the breather they needed to carry Andretti to the win.

At Road America, Unser took advan-

W I N N E R S

It's always upbeat to sketch a group of winners.
Jimmy Vasser can't seem to settle for anything else.
My friend Chip Ganassi was a winner going back to when I sketched him as a driver.
The Italian Alex Zanardi looks the part of a winner as well as being one
and Joe Montana, a subject of mine in numerous Superbowl paintings during
his brilliant football career now adds his winning touch to
auto racing - and this composition.

Le Roy Neiman   1996

tage of some undisciplined driving by the top qualifiers - and some botched pit strategy by the Rahal and Target/Ganassi teams - to take a lead he looked like fashioning into a victory until his Mercedes-Benz blew up on the final lap.

Unser was handicapped by a Penske chassis that was fine on short ovals - of which there were two in 1996 - but hard to consistently balance on road and street circuits. Thus he was forced to fight a strategic battle race after race through mid-season, picking up thirds and fourths when he could. Out of necessity, he also took some un-Unser-like chances at Detroit and Mid-Ohio that ended with the Marlboro Penske parked along the roadside.

Christian Fittipaldi also did an admirable job in a winless season. Many figured he would spend 1996 in Andretti's shadow at Newman-Haas, but that was not the case. While Andretti was bouncing off various Reynards and Penskes in March and April, Fittipaldi was steadily scoring points. He was brilliant at Detroit, scything through the Firestone brigade to take a lead he looked like keeping before a slight bobble after a restart opened the door for Andretti. He also showed a clean pair of heels to Andretti at Road America before the Budweiser Lola Ford suffered an engine failure. But for Road America and an earlier DNF after a coming together with Greg Moore at Long Beach, Christian earned points in every race. And as if the effectiveness of the Andretti/Fittipaldi relationship needed amplification, it was Christian who dutifully moved over on the final lap of the season to enable the Nazarene to clinch second in the points.

In contrast, Andre Ribeiro earned the second and third wins of his IndyCar career with Tasman Motorsports' LCI Lola-Honda in a season marked by inconsistency. He scored a colossally popular victory on home ground at Rio after a long battle with Moore, Johnstone, de Ferran, and Zanardi; came within a splash-and-go of winning the U.S. 500, then atoned for that disappointment by outlasting defending race champion Scott Pruett to win the Michigan 500. But Ribeiro could be as erratic as he was fast. Although he looked like a winner at Detroit before the rains came and at Toronto until a fluffed pit stop, too often his driving showed a desperation that ultimately led to sanctions by IndyCar.

Ribeiro did not want for company on IndyCar's "Most Wanted" list, however. The soul of consistency and restraint in his first season and a half of IndyCar competition, de Ferran seemed to come unglued in July as rumors circulated about the future of the Hall Racing team. Beginning with Cleveland - where he ultimately earned a magnificent victory - de Ferran made contact with competitors on the opening lap in four of the next five races, putting paid to his hopes of winning the PPG Cup for Jim Hall in his final season in racing.

Similarly, Greg Moore began the season looking like the greatest find since Unser and Andretti, and ended it looking distinctly human. He was fast enough at Homestead to unlap himself after a stop-and-go and might have won the race had it been a 300 miler; he had Rio in the bag until suffering an electrical problem and was in the thick of things at the U.S. 500 - despite a 200 mph spin - before blowing an engine. But like de Ferran, he began pressing. He took out Ribeiro at Detroit, got involved with Emerson Fittipaldi at the start of the Michigan 500, tagged Ribeiro again at Mid-Ohio, and then had a third run-in with the Tasman Lola at Road America at upwards of 180 mph, earning the wrath of the IndyCar stewards.

Paul Tracy was another driver to run afoul of officialdom during a bruising, disappointing season. While there's no question Tracy dominated the opening 150 miles at Homestead, there are those who place the blame for his transmission failure squarely on his burn-out from pit lane after his second pit stop.

He squandered a similarly comfortable advantage at Nazareth by entering the pits at warp speed, crashed while racing with Unser in practice at the U.S. 500 (putting Roger Penske in the embarrassing situation of apologizing to Hiro Matsushita for the damage Tracy's wayward PC25 subsequently inflicted upon the Panasonic Lola), crashed again practicing for the Michigan 500, then sent Parker Johnstone into a roll trying to pass the Brix-Comptech Reynard on the last lap at Road America - this while a lap down to the Californian.

It was perhaps the final insult for Johnstone, who might have won the Rio and Michigan races but for mechanical failures. Indeed, mechanical failures were an all too common occurrence on the Motorola Reynard-Honda as the team's budget was stretched past the breaking point by mid-season. Thankfully, Johnstone and the team had already

scored a popular second place at Long Beach by that point.

Not all the young IndyCar drivers were hooligans. Case in point, Adrian Fernandez. Under the tutelage of Tasman Motorsports' Steve Horne and race engineer Diane Holl, Fernandez developed steadily in 1996. After some indifferent results in the first half of the year (when he took more than his share of the blame for the U.S. 500 fiasco) Fernandez came on strong. He scored a fine fourth at Detroit in treacherous wet-conditions before putting the most complete race weekend of his IndyCar career together to win the tragic Toronto race. As much as that victory, the fact that apart from Road America and the two Michigan races, Fernandez earned points in every race from April onward is perhaps the best sign that even better things await in 1997.

When the term 'steady' is used with regard to the 1996 PPG Indy Car World Series, the names Bobby Rahal, Bryan Herta, and Scott Pruett come to mind. Rahal and Herta made little noise in the first part of the year as Team Rahal came to grips with its Reynard chassis after a lengthy association with Lola.

Herta finally broke through with a fifth at Cleveland that seemed to open the floodgates: he never finished worse than sixth the rest of the way, and earned a pair of second places at Michigan and Laguna Seca - where he looked the winner until Zanardi's spectacular last lap pass. Rahal, too, came on strong in the latter half of the year. Strong - as always - at Toronto, he also scored a pair of runner-up finishes at Road America and Vancouver.

Pruett's season with Patrick Racing was the mirror image of Team Rahal's campaign. While results were few and far between for Rahal and Herta early, Pruett was a real force in the Spring, and, in fact, was the only driver other than Vasser to lead the PPG Cup standings after taking fourth at Homestead and third at Rio. Although Pruett's best finish was a second at Surfers Paradise, his finest moments came at Michigan where he took the fight to Ribeiro's seemingly superior Honda-powered Lola. But Pruett's Ford-Cosworth XD faltered with the finish line almost in sight, precipitating a later season decline that saw him fall to tenth in the PPG Cup points.

Robby Gordon had a dismal season. Although he pipped Pruett for third place at Homestead, Gordon didn't take another checkered flag until Portland and

Dan Bianchi

1 Worthy Champion... **Jimmy Vasser** won three of the first four races, plus one other. Took Marlboro Pole Award honors at four events. Finished every race, out of the points only once. (154 PPG Cup points)

finished in the points just three more times. Gordon took a verbal poke at Ford as he departed IndyCar racing for the seemingly greener pastures of NASCAR's Sabco Racing and Pontiac. It may ultimately come back to haunt him.

Raul Boesel was another to suffer a miserable season, thanks in part to repeated mechanical failures. Boesel's woes were exaggerated by the fact that he had finally landed one of the prime rides in IndyCar racing - the Team Green seat vacated by the Formula One-bound Jacques Villeneuve after winning the 1995 PPG Cup. But Boesel's difficulties went deeper than the mechancial department. In addition to Villeneuve, Team Green bid race engineer Tony Cicale farewell at the end of 1995. His replacement - Tino Belli - and Boesel never established an effective working relationship.

Ironically, apart from Newman-Haas, some of Ford's brightest moments came courtesy of teams using the long-in-tooth Cosworth XB. Shut out of a deal for front line engines, PacWest Racing relied on XB power in 1996 and were rewarded with their best finishes at Michigan International Speedway, of all places. The fastest of all the IndyCar tracks proved that there is still a place for reliability and a sweet handling chassis as Mauricio Gugelmin finished second in the U.S. 500 and third at the Michigan 500, while teammate Mark Blundell finished fifth and sixth, respectively at the two Michigan events. PacWest struggled early in the season when a series of brake problems climaxed with Blundell slamming the wall at Rio in a vicious accident from which he was indeed fortunate to escape with minor injuries. Later on, the team got its act together and heads into 1997 on an upbeat note putting together deals with Mercedes-Benz and Firestone.

One of the happiest stories of the season involved another Ford-Cosworth XB-powered team, Payton/Coyne Racing. With evergreen Roberto Moreno a last minute choice for the team's lead car, Walter Payton and Dale Coyne enjoyed their finest season of IndyCar racing as the Brazilian came home in the points in three of the first four races, capping it off with a miraculous third place at the U.S. 500 - the team's first podium finish. Alas, reality soon descended on the financially strapped team and it wasn't until Laguna Seca that Moreno earned another point.

If '96 was the finest hour for one of IndyCar's most veteran teams, it may well have marked the end of the road for its most celebrated veteran driver: Emerson Fittipaldi. Like Unser and Tracy, Fittipaldi was off-form with his Hogan-Penske Racing PC25 Mercedes-Benz on the road courses and street circuits, but was competitive on the mile ovals. He qualified an excellent fifth fastest for the Michigan 500, but crashed heavily on the first lap while trying to pass Greg Moore on the outside of turn two. Lucky not to suffer permanent paralysis, Fittipaldi talked openly of retirement during his convalescence. Danish wunderkind Jan Magnussen filled in admirably for Fittipaldi in the final three races of the year. His brief IndyCar career peaked-with an eighth at Laguna Seca before joining Jackie Stewart's new Formula One team.

Stefan Johansson was lucky not to join Fittipaldi on injured reserve after a terrifying accident at Laguna Seca, caused by a collapsed rear wing on the Bettenhausen Racing Reynard. Prior to his shunt, Johansson announced that he was stepping down from the Bettenhausen ride after a season that saw him earn just a handful of top ten finishes, including fourth at Road America.

1996 was a similarly tough season for two of IndyCar's veteran teams - Galles and Scandia Racing. Galles began the year with former motorcycle world champion Eddie Lawson driving its Lola Mercedes-Benz and though he performed well in his rookie season, "Steady" Eddie stepped out of the car at Toronto in favor of Le Mans winner Davy Jones, whose subsequent performances only underlined the fact that Lawson had done an admirable job. The cockpit at Scandia Motorsports was even more of a revolving door, as Marco Greco, Carlos Guerrero, Michel Jourdain, and Eliseo Salazar all served time in the team's Lola Fords to little effect. Although Greco and Salazar were the only drivers to earn points for the team, Jourdain showed the most promise of the bunch.

The Toyota-powered All American Racers and Arciero-Wells teams had understandably modest goals for 1996, the first season of active competition for the Japanese engine maker. In keeping with Dan Gurney's tradition of producing his own Eagle chassis, All American Racers began with a single Eagle MKV for Juan Manuel Fangio, II, then added a second car for P.J. Jones at Milwaukee. Arciero-Wells took the less ambitious tack of fielding a conventional Reynard 96I for Jeff Krosnoff.

Results were, not unexpectedly, few and far between early in the year, but Jones took full advantage of the sloppy conditions at Detroit to come home ninth while Fangio did him one better with an eighth at Road America. Tragically, Krosnoff perished in a horrific accident in the closing stages of the Toronto race, running over the right rear wheel of Johansson at the end of the Lakeshore Boulevard and slamming into a marshall's post, killing corner worker Gary Avrin in the process. Devastated, the Arciero-Wells team skipped the following Michigan 500 but returned with Max Papis in the seat and was rewarded with a ninth place at Road America.

Despite the clear signs of progress, Toyota will have its work cut out in 1997. Honda will not be resting on its laurels, while Mercedes-Benz will be itching to redeem itself after going winless in '96; especially given the fact that they perceptively closed the performance gap to Honda at mid-season. Ford, too, will be a formidable opponent, with the early teething problems of the XD a thing of the past.

The chassis front will be even more interesting in '97, what with the new Swift chassis debuting in the hands of Andretti and Fittipaldi. Swift's David Bruns has been yearning to design an Indy car for years and, in concert with the Newman-Haas brain trust, is likely to produce a very competitive proposition.

Like Mercedes-Benz, Penske is eager to get back in the win column. So much so that they hired Lola designer John Travis at mid-season and spent the early off-season testing a pair of Reynard 96Is. At the same time, Reynard will have the advantage of sheer numbers and the excellent benchmark 96I from which to develop the 97I, while Lola is coming off a very successful season with the T9600 and had already wooed at least one new customer for the coming season in Player's/Forsythe Racing.

Finally, the tire war figures to continue to intensify. Although the Honda engine was surely a plus for the Target/Ganassi, Tasman, Hall, and Brix-Comptech teams in '96, by most estimates the most important variable in any team's engine-chassis-tire package was the tires. Already dizzying, the pace of tire development only figures to accelerate in '97 and the PPG Cup Championship is likely to be determined as much by tires as by the make of the engine and chassis, as well as the talent and skills of the drivers and teams.

Dan Bianchi

2 Winningest Active Driver... **Michael Andretti** overcame slow start, several shunts and probationary period to win five races, the most of any driver in '96, and top the active driver victory list with 35. (132 PPG Cup points)

Dan Bianchi

3 Rapid Rookie... **Alex Zanardi**, a sensation from the start, won three races. Top pole producer with six. '96 Rookie of the Year and candidate for top honors in '97. (132 PPG Cup points)

Dan Bianchi

4 Ultimate IndyCar Driver... **Al Unser Jr**. Only incredibly bad luck kept him out of the winner's circle despite equipment handicaps. Persevered for points and was in the runnng for another PPG Cup right to the last race. (125 PPG Cup points)

5 Swift Sophomore... **Christian Fittipaldi**. Just short of the winner's circle, though occasionally outshone by teammate Andretti. Became an established front runner in his sophomore IndyCar year and a good bet for high honors in 1997. (110 PPG Cup points) Uncle "Emmo" offers advice.

Geoffrey Hewitt

6 Fast Frenchman... **Gil de Ferran**, after coming close in '95, nailed down his first IndyCar victory. With more patience might have had two more wins. Most sought after "free agent" of '96 will go to Walker Racing in '97. (110 PPG Cup points)

Dan Bianchi

7 Very Viable Veteran... **Bobby Rahal**. Another year out of the win column, though tantalizingly close on several occasions. Regular podium appearances show that speed and savvy are still there. (102 PPG Cup points)

Bob Steig

8 Rahal Teammate.... **Bryan Herta**. Long on talent but heretofore short on results. Thrived in Rahal entourage. Had Laguna Seca year end race in hand until last lap. (86 PPG Cup points)

Steve Swope

9 Instant Front Runner... **Greg Moore** started his rookie season brilliantly, slowed by mid-season pressing tactics. Has the potential to be the next great Canadian driver. (84 PPG Cup points)

Dan Bianchi

10 Early Points Leader... **Scott Pruett**. The only driver except Jimmy Vasser to lead in the '96 PPG Cup points chase, was in contention for the title in the early season. On the pole in Detroit, scored a well earned third place in the season finale. (82 PPG Cup points)

Bob Steig

11 Twice Victorious... **Andre Ribeiro** was one of only four multi-race winners in '96, needs only consistency. He's shown with Al Speyer, Firestone's Racing Director. (76 PPG Cup points)

Paul Webb

12 First Time Winner... **Adrian Fernandez** garnered that elusive first win in '96. Additional victories should come easier. (71 PPG Cup points)

Bob Steig

13 CART's Fastest... **Paul Tracy** was unable to capitalize on his speed. (60 PPG Cup points)

Dan Bianchi

Dan Bianchi

15 Exiting Bettenhausen... **Stefan Johansson**, after a disappointing season, announced his departure from Tony Bettenhausen's Alumax backed team. (43 PPG Cup points)

16 Rough Rookie Ride... **Mark Blundell**, previously a Formula One regular, endured a major early season accident, recovered to post some useful results. (41 PPG Cup points)

Geoffrey Hewitt

17 Potential A Plenty... **Parker Johnstone** made the best of a modest budget and equipment restraints. (33 PPG Cup points)

Dan Bianchi

Steve Swope

18 NASCAR Bound... **Robby Gordon** announced before the end of a disappointing season that he was headed for stock car territory in 1997. (29 PPG Cup points)

19 Accident Hurt... **Emerson Fittipaldi's** horrendous crash at Michigan ended his season early. By year's end he had announced no '97 plans. (29 PPG Cup points)

Dan Bianchi

Bob Steig

20 Bike Champion... **Eddie Lawson** seemed to be making good four-wheel progress in PPG Cup circles, was replaced nonetheless. (26 PPG Cup points)

Teams

Cheryl Day Anderson

By David Phillips

The 1996 PPG Indy Car World Series winning team was nearly a decade in the making. After all, it was in 1989 when the Patrick Racing team, in which Chip Ganassi had recently acquired a majority interest, won the Indianapolis 500 and the PPG Indy Car World Series, then disintegrated. Emerson Fittipaldi and Marlboro headed to Penske Racing and Pat Patrick entered into an ill-fated alliance with Alfa Romeo, leaving Ganassi to go it alone with the remnants of the Patrick organization together with sponsorship from Target stores.

It would take Ganassi eight years to assemble the people, equipment, and resources needed to win another PPG Cup. This one under his own name.

Ganassi got the bulk of the Patrick organization's physical assets in the split, along with several key members of the team, including Tom Anderson, Ganassi's choice to manage the reorganized team. That team would go through a troubled development, marked in equal parts by Ganassi's bold strategical moves and the team's inability to take advantage of them.

After his two seasons running with Ilmor-Chevrolet power, Ganassi joined with Newman-Haas Racing in going with the new Ford-Cosworth XB. Although the new engine offered significant advantages in power, packaging, and fuel

efficiency, it was also unproven. And while Newman-Haas went on to win the '93 PPG Cup after a near miss in '92, Ganassi's team failed to win a race.

Undaunted, he forged a partnership with Reynard Racing Cars, Ltd. that would see the ultra-successful British chassis maker enter the IndyCar market in 1994 as the first serious competition to Lola since the late 1980s. Although the move brought Ganassi two wins, like every other team competing in the IndyCar series in '94, Target/Ganassi was powerless in the face of the Marlboro Penske Racing steamroller.

While Ganassi was making daring moves on the equipment front, he was shuffling drivers in and out of the Target sponsored cars at a dizzying pace.

Eddie Cheever, Robby Gordon, and Arie Luyendyk came and went without a victory in four seasons before Michael Andretti and Mauricio Gugelmin arrived at the start of the Reynard era. The association produced a pair of Andretti victories but he subsequently went home to Newman-Haas in 1995 and, with Gugelmin headed to PacWest, Ganassi was left to start from square one. He did so by hiring Bryan Herta, the 1994 Indy Lights champion who had shown abundant promise in a brief campaign in '95 before being sidelined by serious injuries at Toronto. Ganassi also formed an alliance with fellow team owner Jim

Hayhoe that resulted in Hayhoe's driver for the past several seasons - Jimmy Vasser - taking over the second Target/Ganassi entry with additional backing from STP.

Although the cockpit was something of a revolving door, Ganassi was steadily assembling a talented, motivated, and experienced supporting cast. To Anderson's calmly professional influence, Ganassi added veteran Mike Hull as crew chief in 1994 together with race engineer Morris Nunn, who had been an integral part of the Patrick team in 1989, and talented young Julian Robertson who joined the team after a successful apprenticeship at the Lotus Formula One and Simon IndyCar teams. Grant Weaver joined the team in 1994 as chief mechanic on Gugelmin's car and, in the winter of 1995, Robin Hill was named Target/Ganassi's other chief mechanic while veteran Gary Rovazzini managed the team shop on Industrial Boulevard in Indianapolis.

Chip Ganassi made three more significant changes to the team in preparation for the 1996 season, including switches from Ford to Honda and Goodyear to Firestone. After a tempestuous season together, Ganassi and Herta parted company with the former Indy Lights champion headed for Team Rahal, to be replaced by Reynard-protege and Formula One refugee Alex Zanardi.

Ganassi's singular blend of patience and daring was rewarded in 1996 as Vasser won the PPG Cup while Zanardi earned Rookie of the Year honors and tied Andretti for second in the PPG Cup points race. The seasonal totals included seven wins, ten poles, and a total of eleven podium finishes. But perhaps the most important statistic of all was Vasser's 100% finishing record, with sixteen finishes in sixteen starts, all but one in the PPG Cup points.

Unquestionably, a Honda-powered Reynard on Firestone tires was the combination to have in the first half of the season. For that, Vasser and Zanardi can thank Ganassi for putting the right combination together. Equally clear is the fact that the performance advantage enjoyed by the Target/Ganassi drivers narrowed in the heat of summer as Mercedes-Benz and Goodyear closed the gap and the Lola teams found the handle on the T9600 chassis. Yet the Target/Ganassi cars kept scoring points at a steady clip and for that, Vasser in particular, can thank Honda, Reynard, and Firestone - but most of all his crew - for a car that never let him down when it counted.

Although Vasser bolted to a comfortable lead in the PPG Cup points, he would need every one of his sixteen finishes in the face of challenges from Newman-Haas and Marlboro Penske.

Both Newman-Haas and Marlboro Penske Racing overcame slow starts to challenge for the title. In the case of Newman-Haas, the new Ford-Cosworth XD, in what was admittedly a development season, could not initially match the Honda HRH engine, not to mention the Mercedes-Benz IC108.

That should have called for steady performances in the first part of the season, in order to build a foundation from which to challenge for the PPG Cup when the XD gained momentum. Unfortunately, Michael Andretti didn't read the script and got a mere ten points in the early going. In contrast, Christian Fittipaldi was a model of consistency and patience (Long Beach aside) and, in concert with crew chief Colin Duff, race engineer Brian Lisles, and chief mechanic John Simmonds, brought the Budweiser/Texaco Lola home in the top six points in each of the first three races. But the wins Fittipaldi needed to do more than just stay in the championship hunt never quite materialized.

Knowing full well they couldn't challenge the Hondas on horsepower tracks like Surfers Paradise, Long Beach, and Michigan International Speedway, Andretti, race engineer Peter Gibbons, and crew chief mechanic Tim Bumps knew their only hope was to make hay on the handling tracks such as the mile ovals and the tight street circuits. In the Lola T9600 they had a chassis which was a match for the Reynard 96I.

After Andretti's rocky start, the strategy worked nearly to perfection. With team manager Lee White calling the race strategy, Andretti won at Nazareth then took opportunistic wins at Milwaukee and Detroit before scooping up a fourth win at Road America, a classic horsepower circuit if ever there was one, and a dominant victory at Vancouver. But their late bid to wrest the title from Target/Ganassi's grasp fell short when Andretti experienced a troubled weekend at Laguna Seca, passing a cooperative Fittipaldi on the final lap to finish in a dead heat with Zanardi on points and claim second in the PPG Cup points on the basis of five wins, the most of any driver in '96.

Perhaps the biggest news of the season for Newman-Haas concerned their plans for 1997 and beyond. Beginning next year, Newman-Haas will join San Clemente, California-based Swift Engineering in racing Swift's first Indy car chassis. Swift and its talented head designer David Bruns have an enviable record in the junior formulae and most observers expect the Swift Indy car to be a formidable challenger to the likes of Reynard, Lola, Penske, and Eagle.

At Penske, Al Unser Jr. and Paul Tracy had to cope with a Penske PC25 chassis which was difficult to balance over the course of a changing fuel load on the bumpy street circuits and road courses. The Mercedes-Benz was a little shy of Honda in terms of power at first, but by mid-season there was little to choose between the IC108 and the Honda HRH when it came to power, although reliability proved wanting at the crucial moment at Road America.

Tracy had the Homestead race in the bag before falling out with a broken transmission, and was looking good at Nazareth until he ran over several crew members in a pit stop. Similarly, Unser looked like a winner at Milwaukee until a late full course yellow negated the advantage he'd gained by opting for Goodyear's more durable primary tires.

Unser, chief mechanic Richard Buck, and race engineer Grant Newbury soldiered on, picking away at Vasser's PPG Cup points lead throughout the summer on the strength of consistently finishing in the top five. Yet even as Unser was poised to take the championship lead, the team suffered a crushing blow at Road America when his Mercedes-Benz blew up almost in sight of victory.

It was an equally trying season for chief mechanic Jon Bouslog and race engineer Nigel Beresford, first as they watched Tracy fail to capitalize on his early chances, then embark on a string of undisciplined performances that left the fastest man in IndyCar racing out of the top ten in the points standings.

If anything, the fledgling Hogan/Penske Racing team borne of the alliance between Carl Hogan, Roger Penske, and Marlboro Latin America

Dan Bianchi

Gary Gold

endured an even more troubled season. Although Emerson Fittipaldi proved quick on the mile ovals, he was off the pace at most other tracks. Race engineer Tom Brown and chief mechanic Rick Rinaman had the PC25 Mercedes working well in practice and qualifying for the Michigan 500 but Fittipaldi's huge crash on the opening lap brought the Brazilian's season - and possibly his career - to an end. Under the direction of team manager Tom Wurtz, Hogan/Penske regrouped and entered budding Danish superstar Jan Magnussen in the final three events and were rewarded with an eighth place finish at Laguna Seca - the best for a

Penske car in the season finale. With Fittipaldi's return doubtful, Magnussen headed to Jackie Stewart's new Formula One team, and Marlboro Latin America looking elsewhere, there may not be a sophomore season for Hogan/Penske Racing.

If one team appears on the verge of extinction, another whose future seemed in doubt this season has a new lease on life. We're speaking of Hall Racing, which was taken over by team manager Gerald Davis in the wake of Jim Hall's retirement from racing. Davis subsequently secured the support of Vancouver businessman Murray Craig to form Davis-

Craig Racing for 1997 and will continue to work out of the Midland, Texas facility that has served the team well since its inception as Hall/VDS Racing.

Davis-Craig Racing can build on a solid 1996 season, one highlighted by a victory at Cleveland, together with podium finishes at Homestead, Detroit, and Portland. Although driver Gil de Ferran took race engineer Bill Pappas in his post-season move to Walker Racing, the nucleus of the Hall team is back including Davis and chief mechanic Alex Hering. With Indy Lights driver standout Gaulter Salles on board, together with veteran race engineer Chuck Matthews, Davis-Craig's Reynard Ford-Cosworths should carry on the tradition of Hall Racing in fine fashion.

Craig isn't the only new co-owner in the sport. For in the wake of his split with Carl Hogan, Bobby Rahal formed a new partnership with popular late night television talk show host David Letterman. The ownership wasn't the only thing to change at Team Rahal for 1996. With Scott Roembke returning as general manager, Tim Cindric assumed the role of team manager in the wake of Jim Prescott's decision to return to his post as crew chief on Rahal's car. His counterpart, Larry Ellert, found himself working for Bryan Herta after Raul Boesel's surprise departure from the team in November 1995. Race engineers Tim Reiter and Ray Lehto returned for another season with Rahal and Herta, respectively.

Additionally, Team Rahal ended its long relationship with Lola in favor of Reynard chassis for the 1996 season. Some things never change, however, as Miller Brewing continued its long associ-

Bob Steig

ation with Rahal - and will continue to do so at least through the end of the millenium - while Shell Oil came on board as principle sponsor of Herta's car.

Although it took time for the team to adjust to the changes, by mid-season Rahal and Herta had begun to assert themselves and finished the year with a string of podium finishes even if victory, ultimately, eluded them.

Columbus, Ohio's "other team" made it to victory lane on three separate occasions, clear indication of the maturation both of the Tasman Motorsports Group and its two young drivers. That the team also won several races while running a three car team in the PPG Firestone Indy Lights Championship underscores Tasman's emerging strength in just its fourth year of existence.

As usual Steve Horne and co-owner-team manager Jeff Eischen were in charge of operations, while race engineer Don Halliday returned for his fourth season with the team, his third straight working with Andre Ribeiro, together with chief mechanic Steve Ragan. Adrian Fernandez was a late addition to the team, and Tasman quickly enlisted former Reynard engineer Diane Holl to work alongside chief mechanic Ed Daood as race engineer on the Mexican's Tecate Lola Honda. The line up produced a pair of wins for Ribeiro and his LCI Lola Honda in the Rio 400 and the Michigan 500 while Fernandez scored a win at Toronto in a season that saw him finish all but five races in the points.

The Player's/Forsythe and Patrick Racing teams came about as close to winning as possible without actually mounting the top rung of the podium. Gerry Forsythe's association with Player's paid dividends when the Canadian tobacco company brought 1995 Indy Lights champion Greg Moore - together with longtime friend and race engineer Steve Chalis - to the team over the winter. Just 20 years old at the beginning of the season, Moore took to Indy cars immediately and might have won the first two races but for jumping a restart at Homestead and an electrical failure while leading at Rio. Although Moore had his ups and downs later in the year, he has already staked a claim as an IndyCar "Star of Tomorrow" and will return for a second season a year older and very much the wiser.

Even if their IndyCar team fell just shy of victory in 1996, Forsythe and vice president of operations Neil Mickelwright

could take pride in the fact that their team won its second straight PPG Firestone Indy Lights title thanks to the efforts of David Empringham.

Under the leadership of general manager Jim McGee and team manager Steve Newey, and with Scott Pruett at the wheel of their Lola Ford, Patrick Racing seemed poised to make a run at the PPG Cup in the early stages of the season. Together with race engineer Tom German, crew chief Tony Van Dongen and chief mechanic Mike Sales, Pruett and the Patrick team were a formidable

Geoffrey Hewitt

force in March and April, scoring three top four finishes in the opening races and going on to earn pole and outside front row starting spots at Detroit and Portland, respectively. A series of DNFs at mid-year - culminating in a blown engine in the closing stages of the Michigan 500 - took the wind out of the team's sails. But Pruett finished off the season with a third place at Laguna Seca to secure the team's second straight top ten finish in the PPG Cup Championship.

Brix-Comptech Racing was another team to come tantalizingly close to victory, but like Player's/Forsythe and Patrick Racing, had to settle for second place as their highwater mark. 1996 marked the second season of Harry Brix's partnership with Comptech owners Doug Peterson and Don Erb, a partnership that again brought sponsorship from Motorola to the party. Veteran race engineer Ed Nathman came to the team from Galles Racing and, together with chief mechanic Barry Brooke and the gregarious Parker Johnstone, formed the backbone of the team. Though Johnstone looked a potential winner at Rio and the U.S. 500, his best finish would come at Long Beach where he held off a late charge by the King of the Beach - Al Unser Jr. - to finish second.

PacWest Racing was another team to make it to the second rung of the podium, thanks to Mauricio Gugelmin's remarkable run to second place in the U.S. 500, a feat he nearly duplicated later in the Michigan 500 when he brought the Hollywood Reynard Ford home in third place. Those finishes were highlights of a season marked by growing pains for the team, now in its fourth season, owned by Bruce McCaw, Tom Armstrong, Dominic Dobson, and Wes Lamatta. 1996 saw PacWest bring in Formula One refugee Mark Blundell to partner Gugelmin under the direction of team manager John Anderson, together with chief mechanics Paul Harcus and Russ Cameron and race engineer Andy Brown. Blundell got off to a horrendous start, crashing heavily in Brazil and missing the next two races as a result, but rebounded with a fifth at the U.S. 500 in the VISA Reynard, later matching that finish in Detroit.

PacWest finished the season with a couple of major announcements, namely switching from Goodyear to Firestone tires and from Ford-Cosworth to Mercedes-Benz power in preparation for what figures to be a crucial season of racing for the team.

The high banks at Michigan International Speedway also favored Payton-

Dan Bianchi

Sophomore Season... Dan Gurney's All American Racer team heads into the second year of its return to the Indy car racing wars with further developed versions of the Toyota engines that debuted in '96 and a new chassis choice, Reynard. His drivers, Juan Manuel Fangio II and P.J. Jones, have rookie years behind them and are looking to translate their experience into meaningful PPG Cup points production in '97.

Coyne Racing as Roberto Moreno brought the team's Lola Ford home third in the U.S. 500, marking the first trip to the podium for owners Dale Coyne and Walter Payton. The U.S. 500 was also a

Cheryl Day Anderson

long overdue reward for crew chief Bernie Myers and the remainder of the team who have spent countless hours preparing the team's cars over the years. It was not, however, the only time the team finished in the PPG Cup points for Moreno brought the Data Control Lola home in the top twelve on his home ground at Rio as well as in Australia and Long Beach, while Hiro Matsushita scored points in Australia with a tenth place finish in the Panasonic Lola.

For their troubles Payton, Coyne, and Moreno outscored some rather more high profiled teams. Defending PPG Cup Champion Team Green along with owner Barry Green, team manager Kim Green, and chief mechanic Tony Cottman had a rebuilding year, having lost star driver Jacques Villeneuve to Formula One. His replacement, Raul Boesel, finished just five times, and was frequently off the pace in the Brahma Sports Reynard. In part their difficulties could be traced to a series of mechanical problems, but also to the fact that Boesel and race engineer Tino Belli failed to match the chemistry that existed on the team in the glory

days of Villeneuve and engineer Tony Cicale.

Derrick Walker's team fared little better, as Robby Gordon got the season off to a good start with a third at Homestead but never came close to the podium again. In a disappointing season, like Boesel and Belli, Gordon and race engineer Lee Dykstra never clicked; nor, after Dykstra headed to greener pastures, did Gordon and Rob Edwards make any discernible headway with the Valvoline Reynard. Formula 3000 veteran Ron Meadows was recruited to manage what was expected to be a two car team for the balance of the season, but Scott Goodyear suffered serious back injuries in Rio and only made three more appearances, which included a ninth at Vancouver.

Next season sees Gil de Ferran joining Valvoline's standard bearing IndyCar team, together with ex-Hall Racing engineer Bill Pappas. With Honda power in the mix as well, Walker should have everything he needs to get back to the front of the pack.

Bettenhausen Racing is another team which will have a new look in '97, as Toyota Atlantic champion Patrick Carpentier fills the vacancy created when Stefan Johansson decided to step down from the team after a disappointing

1996 campaign. Johansson was frustrated to earn just three top six finishes with a team that, seemingly, had the right people and the right equipment in place. Team manager Martin Dixon was back for another season, together with veteran chief mechanic Joe Ward and race engineer Bernie Marcus, while Bettenhausen had acquired a brace of new Reynard 96Is after spending the last few seasons fighting an uphill battle with year old Penskes. But the combination never reached its potential, and Johansson's top finishes resulted more from the reliability of the Alumax Reynard Mercedes-Benz than speed.

1996 likely also marked the end of the line in the PPG Indy Car World Series for two of IndyCar's veteran teams - Galles and Scandia Racing - both of which are headed to the rival Indy Racing League in 1997. Galles began the season with high hopes, having made the intriguing choice of former World Champion motorcyclist and Indy Lights winnner Eddie Lawson as driver of his Delco Electronics Lola Mercedes-Benz. Veteran team manager Owen Snyder was back on board together with chief mechanic Gary Armentrout but the team went through a number of race engineers before settling on Gary Grossenbacher. Despite several promising showings, Lawson opted to stand down from the team after Toronto. After his replacement - Davy Jones - finished in the points only once, Galles turned his sights on the IRL for 1997.

If anything, the cockpit at Team Scandia was even more of a revolving door as Eliseo Salazar, Carlos Guerrero, Marco Greco, and Michel Jourdain all did time in the Lola Fords owned by Andy and Ann Evans, who acquired controlling interest in the team from Dick and Diane Simon in the off-season. Simon stayed on to oversee the engineering duties while veteran team manager Gilbert Lage and crew chief John Weland were also on hand, but results were few and far between, leading Evans to pursue the IRL in '97.

But the door between the PPG Indy Car World Series and the Indy Racing League swings both ways, as Della Penna Motorsports proved. A veteran team owner in Toyota Atlantic, John Della Penna decided the time was right this year to move his team and 1995 Toyota Atlantic champ Richie Hearn to IndyCar. While running the full IRL schedule, Della Penna participated in the Long Beach, Toronto, and Laguna Seca

Steve Swope

IndyCar races, with Hearn earning a tenth place finish at Long Beach in an updated 1995 Reynard prepared by crew chief Brendon Cleave and engineered by David Cripps. After Della Penna revealed that his team would run the full PPG Cup schedule in 1997, Hearn went on to win the final IRL event of the 1996 calendar year at Las Vegas Motor Speeday.

Hearn and the Della Penna team will have to step things up several notches if they are to enjoy similar success in the 1997 PPG Indy Car World Series. So, too, will Arciero-Wells Racing and All American Racers as they enter a second season with Toyota power. Arciero-Wells endured the sad loss of driver Jeff Krosnoff in an accident in the closing laps at Toronto, but owners Frank and Albert Arciero and Cal Wells III, pulled things together in time for the final three races of the season. They hired Max Papis to replace Krosnoff and, under the guidance of team manager Bob Sprow and engineer Gordon Coppuck, the mercurial Italian quickly established himself in the PPG Indy Car World Series with several strong qualifying performances

and an outstanding ninth place at Road America.

1996 also marked the welcome return of Dan Gurney and his All American Racers to IndyCar competition. Like Arciero-Wells' Reynard Toyota, the All American Racer effort was based on a brand new engine throughout the season. All American Racer's task was made more difficult by the fact that Gurney & Co. were also running a chassis of their own design, the Eagle MKV.

All American Racers began the season as a one car operation for former Camel GT champion Juan Manuel Fangio II under the direction of team manager Gary Donahoe and prepared by crew chief Gary Martin, then added a second Eagle for P.J. Jones beginning at Milwaukee. The Toyota's maiden year made the performance of the Castrol sponsored Eagles difficult to evaluate, but the fact that they were regularly outqualified by Papis' Reynard by the end of the season (albeit with the MCI entry on Firestones and the AAR cars on Goodyears) suggested that the team's chassis were somewhat short of the

mark as well. This conclusion was supported by the fact that Gurney and designer John Ward parted company at season's end, with Gurney testing the proven Reynard chassis for possible use in '97.

Altogether, 1996 saw no fewer than 17 drivers finish on the podium with six different winners, three of them first time IndyCar winners. Two of the four manufacturers of chassis and engines won races (and Penske and Mercedes-Benz came achingly close to making it three of four in both cases). Both Firestone and Goodyear made it to victory lane, with Firestone claiming bragging rights with the higher point total.

The 1997 season promises more close competition between evenly matched drivers, chassis, engines, and tires. Next year will also see the introduction of two exciting new venues to the PPG Indy Car World Series in Gateway International Raceway near St. Louis and California Speedway in Fontana, California, with the awesome Twin Ring Motegi circuit in Japan slated for Spring of 1998.

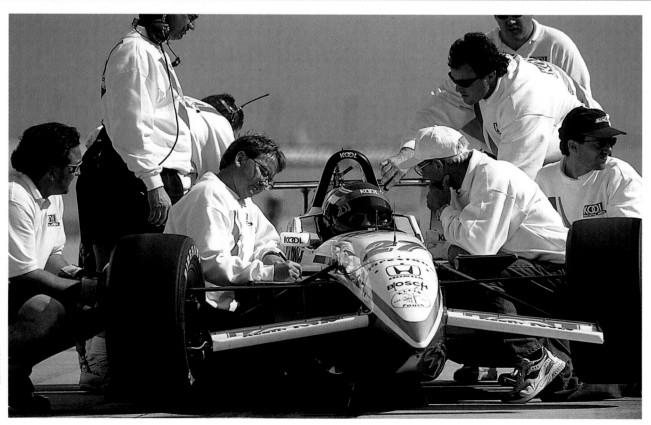

Team KOOL Green
Goes for the Gold
- Again

Winner of the '95 PPG Cup with star driver Jacques Villeneuve, team owner Barry Green had the unenviable task of rebuilding in '96. Villeneuve left to follow in his charismatic father's Formula One footsteps. His departure left a void too deep to fill quickly. With the '97 season on hand, however, the rejuvenation is well under way. Green has a major new sponsor, KOOL, a new equipment package, the Reynard-Honda-Firestone combination that took Target/Ganassi to first and a tie for second in the PPG Cup points in '96, and a new driver, Parker Johnstone. Johnstone earned his Indy car spurs with a second tier team, looks forward to his first season with one of CART's elite organizations. He's fast (has a 230 mph pole in his logbook), personable - and an American, all requirements in Team KOOL Green's off-season talent search. There's even an important old ingredient. Missing in '96, Tony Cicale, the aerodynamics genius behind Villeneuve's rise, is back in the harness, lured by the prospect of winning another PPG Cup. Cicale's "low downforce" approach, which puts more of the cornering burden on the driver, should suit Johnstone just fine.

Dan Bianchi

1996 PPG Indy Car World Series Driver Performance Chart

Rank	Driver	Pts.	Starts	Run at Finish	Top Finish	Times Led	Laps Led	Laps Comp.	Miles Comp.
1	JIMMY VASSER	154	16	16	1	12	162	1990	3637.606
2	MICHAEL ANDRETTI	132	16	10	1	10	281	1571	2777.955
3	ALEX ZANARDI	132	16	10	1	26	610	1563	2838.807
4	AL UNSER JR.	125	16	13	2	5	125	1967	3581.396
5	CHRISTIAN FITTIPALDI	110	16	13	2	3	80	1913	3494.381
6	GIL DE FERRAN	104	16	11	1	6	172	1741	3105.203
7	BOBBY RAHAL	102	16	12	2	1	1	1618	2867.994
8	BRYAN HERTA	86	16	13	2	2	41	1839	3327.557
9	GREG MOORE	84	16	9	2	8	73	1691	3008.895
10	SCOTT PRUETT	82	16	11	2	4	12	1613	2895.096
11	ANDRE RIBEIRO	76	16	9	1	6	166	1759	3167.517
12	ADRIAN FERNANDEZ	71	15	13	1	2	17	1602	2822.055
13	PAUL TRACY	60	14	8	3	5	214	1342	2296.901
14	MAURICIO GUGELMIN	53	16	10	2	3	12	1625	2898.054
15	STEFAN JOHANSSON	43	16	8	4	0	0	1605	3040.480
16	MARK BLUNDELL	41	13	9	5	0	0	1386	2574.251
17	PARKER JOHNSTONE	33	15	7	2	2	35	1597	2878.186
18	ROBBY GORDON	29	16	9	3	1	2	1669	2995.048
19	EMERSON FITTIPALDI	29	12	5	4	0	0	1191	1879.116
20	EDDIE LAWSON	26	11	9	6	0	0	1282	2118.777
21	ROBERTO MORENO	25	15	7	3	1	2	1334	2455.578
22	RAUL BOESEL	17	16	5	7	0	0	1368	2479.844
23	JUAN MANUEL FANGIO II	5	16	7	8	0	0	1299	2436.455
24	JAN MAGNUSSEN	5	4	2	8	0	0	212	448.821
25	SCOTT GOODYEAR	5	4	4	9	0	0	400	708.153
26	P.J. JONES	4	10	5	9	0	0	792	1428.293
27	MAX PAPIS	4	3	1	9	0	0	129	376.332
28	HIRO MATSUSHITA	3	16	7	10	0	0	1261	2544.520
29	RICHIE HEARN	3	3	2	10	0	0	233	432.010
30	ELISEO SALAZAR	2	4	4	11	0	0	603	1036.650
31	DAVY JONES	1	5	4	12	0	0	515	1066.007
32	MARCO GRECO	1	2	1	12	0	0	195	341.912
33	CARLOS GUERRERO	0	3	1	14	0	0	255	482.216
34	MIKE GROFF	0	1	1	14	0	0	192	192.000
35	JEFF KROSNOFF	0	11	4	15	0	0	1060	1724.955
36	TEO FABI	0	2	1	16	0	0	274	324.740
37	MICHEL JOURDAIN JR.	0	5	1	16	0	0	384	543.653
38	DENNIS VITOLO	0	1	0	17	0	0	87	138.330
39	GARY BETTENHAUSEN	0	1	0	21	0	0	79	158.000
40	FREDRIK EKBLOM	0	1	0	25	0	0	11	22.000

1996 PPG Cup Point Fund

JIMMY VASSER, $1,000,000; MICHAEL ANDRETTI, $500,000; ALEX ZANARDI, $300,000; AL UNSER JR., $200,000; CHRISTIAN FITTIPALDI, $150,000; GIL DE FERRAN, $140,000; BOBBY RAHAL, $130,000; BRYAN HERTA, $120,000; GREG MOORE, $110,000; SCOTT PRUETT, $100,000

Cheryl Day Anderson

PPG Indy Car World Series Race 1
Marlboro Grand Prix of Miami
Presented by Toyota
Homestead Motorsports Complex
Homestead, Florida
March 3, 1996
133 Laps, 1.5 Mile Oval

MIAMI GOES TO FIRST TIME WINNER JIMMY VASSER

Almost a winner back in June of 1995 at Portland's Budweiser/G.I. Joe's 200, Jimmy Vasser made it stick this time, earning his first PPG Cup victory with 3.156 seconds in hand over runner-up Gil de Ferran.

As Vasser and others would demonstrate throughout the season, the Reynard/Honda/Firestone package, meticulously prepared for him by his Target/Ganassi team was the combination to beat in 1996. Polesitter Paul Tracy did just that for 83 laps, building up a sizeable lead despite multiple caution flags, including a first lap shunt between Michael Andretti and Mauricio Gugelmin and a drizzle induced red flag, which called for a restart. Tracy's colorful Marlboro car with Mercedes-Benz power and Goodyear tires in Penske's own PC96 chassis ground to a halt shortly thereafter due to transmission failure. De Ferran, the second fastest qualifier, inherited the lead, with Vasser, who qualified in the third slot, in avid pursuit. When Andre Ribeiro

and Robby Gordon tangled on lap 82, Vasser timed the restart on lap 101 perfectly and got by de Ferran, cleanly, for a lead he would never relinquish.

Gordon survived his tangle with Ribeiro little the worse for wear and nailed down third place in his Valvoline/Cummins/Craftsman Reynard with Ford-Cosworth power. Scott Pruett and Bobby Rahal matched their respective fourth and fifth starting positions by finishing in the same order. Canadian Greg Moore notched rookie honors with a seventh place finish.

With his maiden voyage to the winner's circle smoothly completed, Vasser can be expected to exploit his advantage and make a serious run at the PPG Cup.

PPG Indy Car World Series Race 2
Rio 400
Emerson Fittipaldi Speedway
Rio de Janeiro, Brazil
March 17, 1996
133 Laps, 1.6 Mile Oval

BRAZILIAN ANDRE RIBEIRO TAKES THE INAUGURAL RIO 400

Cheered on by a wildly enthusiastic "hometown" crowd of 75,000 at Rio de Janeiro's new Emerson Fittipaldi Speedway oval, Andre Ribeiro turned the inaugural Rio 400 into a high decibel Brazilian festival with his highly popular win. Ribeiro was stalked for every one of the last 18 laps he led by the driver nobody wants to see in his mirrors, Al Unser

Jr. Unser's best efforts were unavailing. Despite a restart with four laps to go, due to a Robby Gordon single car accident, Unser had to settle for second place, 2.141 seconds back. Firestone standard bearer Scott Pruett nailed down third place, leaving him atop the PPG Cup standings, a single point over today's eighth place finisher, Jimmy Vasser, the winner of the season opener. As the PPG Cup campaign unfolded, this would be the only time all year that Vasser would not hold the points lead, albeit somewhat precariously at times. Polesitter Alex Zanardi, Vasser's Target/Ganassi teammate, held the lead on three occasions for a total of 64 laps out front, finished fourth. The Italian ex-Formula One driver served strong notice of exciting results to come. Christian Fittipaldi made a big move up from his 27th starting place to finish fourth,

followed by Bobby Rahal and Raul Boesel.

Gil de Ferran, who took over the lead from Zanardi, looked like a winner for his 20 laps out in front but ran out of fuel and was lucky to make it back to the pits. The misadventure cost him two laps. Another rookie, Canadian Greg Moore, in the Player's/Indeck Reynard, had a heady turn in the point position, only to be felled by engine failure on lap 116 of the 133 scheduled.

Ribeiro, the LCI-backed driver who had been in the hunt all day, inherited the lead and held off Unser for the 18 laps remaining. Brazilian national hero Emerson Fittipaldi had the rare privilege of starting a major race on a new speedway named for him. It would be nice to report that he had been battling the leaders all the way, but he finished just outside the first ten.

PPG Indy Car World Series Race 3
IndyCar Australia
Surfers Paradise
Queensland, Australia
March 31, 1996
65 Laps, 2.804 Mile Road Course

JIMMY VASSER WINS INDYCAR AUSTRALIA FROM THE POLE

Only five of the 65 laps around the beautiful Surfers Paradise street circuit were led by any driver other than Jimmy Vasser, who won in dominating fashion. His Target/Ganassi Reynard Honda was headed for this short period by Scott Pruett's Firestone Lola Ford, which ended up in second place after starting alongside Vasser on the outside pole. On the mechanical side, the race represented a sweep of the first three events by the Reynard/Honda/Firestone combination. Greg Moore, in the Player's/Forsythe/Indeck Reynard made his first ever IndyCar podium finish, taking third place, and demoting rival Alex Zanardi to second place in the battle for Rookie of the Year honors. Zanardi got off to a good start from his third qualifying position, but lost his battle with transmission problems after only 31 laps. Mauricio Gugelmin and Christian Fittipaldi occupied the next two finishing positions while Stefan Johansson, in the Alumax Reynard, took down the sixth spot, his best finish of the year.

Vasser called his Firestone-shod Reynard Honda, "The most beautiful race car I ever had. It ran like clockwork all day and made my job easy." What didn't make it easy was a fuel overflow problem that left him with less than full tanks after his first two pit stops, and made an extra stop, happily under caution, necessary. Vasser handled even this problem with despatch.

Paul Webb

PPG Indy Car World Series Race 4
Toyota Grand Prix of Long Beach
Long Beach, California
April 14, 1996
105 Laps, 1.59 Mile Road Course

TOYOTA GRAND PRIX OF LONG BEACH FALLS TO JIMMY VASSER

At Long Beach, a streaking Jimmy Vasser made it three wins out of the first four IndyCar races of the new season, an incredible .750 average. This one he owed to luck; bad for Gil de Ferran, who put his Pennzoil Reynard Honda on the pole, and led 100 of the 105 laps contested. Good for Vasser, who picked up the win when de Ferran's turbo-charger hose detached with four laps remaining. Bad luck, too, visited second fastest qualifier Alex Zanardi, who crashed after taking the lead on lap 39. Race runner-up Parker Johnstone, in the Motorola Reynard Honda, was thrilled to beat his youthful hero Al Unser Jr., the third place finisher, at one of Unser's favorite tracks. Johnstone, enjoying his best ever IndyCar finish, had no realistic shot at catching Vasser, but held off Unser in workmanlike fashion. Marlboro Team Penske's fortunes, showing improvement, gained with Paul Tracy's fourth place finish.

Christian Fittipaldi's lap 48 tangle with rookie Greg Moore had a second round after the two disabled cars came to a halt. Fittipaldi went over to Moore's car and half-pulled him out by the visor, netting himself a $5,000 unsportsmanlike conduct fine. Scott Pruett, off the podium for the first time in 1996, scored a couple of points for an 11th place finish. His 44 point total was sufficient to maintain second place in the PPG Cup title chase, behind leader Vasser with 67 and ahead of perennial top contender Unser in third place with 39. Luck or not, Vasser appears to have a sensational year well started. Not since Mario Andretti in 1985, had any driver taken three of the first four events. Despite his fast start, Andretti failed to take the title.

Cheryl Day Anderson

Nazareth

Bob Steig

PPG Indy Car World Series Race 5
Bosch Spark Plug Grand Prix
Nazareth Speedway
Nazareth, Pennsylvania
April 28, 1996
200 Laps, 1 Mile Oval

MICHAEL ANDRETTI BOUNCES BACK IN NAZARETH

Michael Andretti, the Kmart Texaco-Havoline standard bearer, who, unaccountably, had been bouncing around in midfield, bounced back to the top of the heap in Nazareth, his hometown. He and his Newman-Haas teammates heaved an audible sigh of relief, as did the Lola/Ford/Goodyear contingent, all racking up their first win of the year. Andretti led the last 113 laps, after taking over from polesitter Paul Tracy, the leader for the first 87 laps. No other driver was able to poke a nose in front.

Rookie Greg Moore was a substantial 12.213 seconds behind the flying Andretti at the finish. Al Unser Jr., still seeking a '96 victory, made another podium appearance in third place, and notched second place in the PPG Cup standings. Points leader Jimmy Vasser qualified well (third place) but finished seventh. He stayed well out in front in total points with 73. Eighth place today for Scott Pruett bumped him back to third in the PPG Cup title chase with 49 points. Emerson Fittipaldi, responding to a track he likes, put in his best effort of the new season, qualifying second and finishing fourth. Tracy's brilliant early effort faded in the second half of the race, but helped earn him the fifth finishing position. Bobby Rahal sandwiched his Miller Reynard in between Paul Tracy and Jimmy Vasser at the end. The big item of the Nazareth outing was the return to winning ways of a great driver who had labored out of the limelight earlier in the season. Having found his way back to victory circle, most veteran observers expect Andretti to make repeat visits as the season unfolds.

PPG Indy Car World Series Race 6
U.S. 500
Michigan International Speedway
Brooklyn, Michigan
May 26, 1996
250 Laps, 2 Mile Oval

JIMMY VASSER WINS BIZARRE INAUGURAL U.S. 500 AND $1 MILLION

Hollywood would reject the script... *Likeable polesitter triggers big 12 car accident on the first lap of the season's richest race, escapes unscathed, goes on to glory and $1 million plus payday in back up car.* Jimmy Vasser, ever the good soldier, took the role anyway, and was amply rewarded. Marlboro had posted a special $100,000 pole award, and added a $45,000 bonus for winning from the pole, making Vasser's post race trip to the bank a particularly happy one. Although almost half the field was involved, incredibly, no driver was hurt in the huge first lap pile up. All except one, second fastest qualifier Adrian Fernandez, were able to take the restart in back up cars or repaired primary racers, after a one hour delay. The restart saw everyone except the unfortunate Fernandez in his original starting position. Jimmy Vasser led the first

18 laps before giving way to fourth fastest qualifier Alex Zanardi. Mauricio Gugelmin and Roberto Moreno were out in front for short stints before Zanardi took over again with a very impressive performance, notching 127 laps in the lead. He was sidelined by engine failure on lap 176, after looking like a winner.

Four drivers exchanged the lead over the final 87 laps. Of the four, only Vasser didn't run afoul of misfor-tune. Rookie Greg Moore survived a spinout on lap 160 but couldn't over-come engine problems. Parker Johnstone ran out of fuel on the course, as did Andre Ribeiro, allow-ing Vasser to motor home comfort-ably by 10.995 seconds over second place finisher Mauricio Gugelmin in the Hollywood PacWest Reynard Ford. In his best outing to date, Roberto Moreno occupied the third chair on the winner's podium.

Vasser and the Target/Ganassi team again combined good fortune, good preparation, and a "can do" attitude into the biggest win on the PPG Cup circuit, even if Hollywood wouldn't buy the script. Though Jimmy Vasser's winning percentage was now a mere .666, his 94 PPG Cup points dwarfed second place Al Unser Jr.'s 58 and third place Scott Pruett's 49. Unser was eighth today and Pruett an early dropout.

U.S. 500

Michael C. Brown

Dan Bianchi

Godfather of Indy Car Racing...Jim Chapman, PPG Industries' long term Racing Director, and father figure to many in the sport, lost his bout with cancer in October. He will long be remembered as the creator of the PPG Indy Car World Series, which married two powerful but often divergent bodies, Championship Auto Racing Teams and the Indianapolis Motor Speedway. PPG provided an annual multimillion dollar dowry. The union was key to the blossoming of the sport and its current huge success. A retired Chapman lived to witness the divorce of the two entities, with the Indianapolis 500 becoming part of the new Indy Racing League and Championship Auto Racing Teams developing a rival U.S. 500 as part of their renamed PPG CART World Series. To the end, he remained the friend and confidant of both sides, a posture as unique as the man himself.

Steve Swope

PPG Indy Car World Series Race 7
Miller 200
The Milwaukee Mile
West Allis, Wisconsin
June 2, 1996
200 Laps, 1 Mile Oval

MICHAEL ANDRETTI'S MILWAUKEE VICTORY MAKES HIM THE WINNINGEST ACTIVE DRIVER

Michael Andretti's win in the Miller 200 was doubly delicious. He passed perennial rival Al Unser Jr. on the last restart to beat him to the checker by a scant .146 seconds, admittedly with the help of two caution flags in the last five laps. Moreover, Andretti broke a tie with Unser to become the winningest active IndyCar driver with 32 first place finishes. Andretti also relaunched himself into the '96 PPG Cup title chase with a new total of 51 points behind second place Unser with 75 and leader Jimmy Vasser with 97. Not exactly close but within striking distance with nine events yet to come. Third finisher Paul Tracy, Unser's stablemate, started from the pole, added to a good day for Marlboro Team Penske, albeit one short of victory. No driver other than the top three finishers ever made it to the front, although Emerson Fittipaldi in the Marlboro Hogan Penske made a good effort. He qualified second and finished fourth. Greg Moore, Christian Fittipaldi, the third fastest qualifier, Bobby Rahal, Andre Ribeiro, Gil de Ferran, and Jimmy Vasser rounded out the top ten. A record crowd was treated to some classic short oval racing by three of the masters of this demanding discipline. Keeping the crowd out of their seats, the trio exchanged the lead six times, with Andretti on top when it counted.

PPG Indy Car World Series Race 8
ITT Automotive Detroit Grand Prix
The Raceway on Belle Isle
Detroit, Michigan
June 9, 1996
72 Laps, 2.1 Mile Road Course

**ANDRETTI DOES IT AGAIN
WINS
DETROIT GRAND PRIX
ON LATE RACE PASS**

This time the victim of Michael Andretti's finely honed passing talent was his own Newman-Haas teammate, Christian Fittipaldi. Fittipaldi, in the Kmart/Budweiser Lola Ford, owned the race until a late race caution, triggered by Bobby Rahal's trip into a tire barrier on lap 61, allowed Andretti to catch up. Michael Andretti, in the Kmart Texaco-Havoline Lola, made a clean pass on lap 66, aided by a slight

Fittipaldi miscue. Once in the lead, Andretti cruised to the checker six laps later. Up til that point Fittipaldi had a substantial margin over the field, leading every lap except the first. This went to polesitter Scott Pruett, the Firestone standard bearer. Rain was the order of the weekend but, incredibly, the skies cleared by the start of the race. The still soaked track called for rain tires for the first 25 laps, at which point the

field switched to slicks. The wet early conditions, and six caution flags dropped the winning average speed to just over 75 mph. In addition to Rahal, Al Unser Jr. made a rare barrier contact, as did Andre Ribeiro, Emerson Fittipaldi, and Robby Gordon, the winner here in 1995. Gordon put his Valvoline/Cummins Reynard out of action after only three laps. Understandably, winner Andretti's probationary status, meted

out by CART officials after the Toyota Grand Prix of Long Beach, was lifted after the race. While on probation Andretti won three out of the next four races. "He's been an honor student since he's been on probation," said IndyCar chief steward Wally Dallenbach in his announcement. "With the kind of luck he's been having he might prefer to stay on."

Gil de Ferran took the third podium position after a strong run

from his seventh starting slot. P.J. Jones put his All American Racers Toyota powered Eagle into the top ten, a first for Dan Gurney's new team. PPG Cup points leader Jimmy Vasser struggled, but registered a single point, upping his total to 98 points, 23 more than Unser at 75. Andretti left with 71 points and a new degree of confidence that augured well for the PPG Indy Car World Series championship battle ahead.

Cheryl Dav Anderson

PPG Indy Car World Series Race 9
Budweiser/G.I.Joe's 200
Presented by Texaco-Havoline
Portland International Raceway
Portland, Oregon
June 23, 1996
98 Laps, 1.95 Mile Road Course

PORTLAND FALLS TO ALEX ZANARDI HIS FIRST INDYCAR VICTORY

Italy's Alex Zanardi, an IndyCar rookie but hardly a novice, took his first victory on the PPG Cup circuit in style, winning from the pole and posting a convincing 9.137 second margin over second place Gil de Ferran. Zanardi, a front runner since his debut, took the pole at Rio in March, has been knocking at the door all season. He was the first Italian to win an IndyCar race since Teo Fabi in 1989. Zanardi led all but three of the scheduled 98 laps, at one point enjoyed an advantage of almost half a minute. Tire strategy played a major role in his victory. Despite the intermittent rain he opted to stay out on Firestone slicks. Al Unser Jr. who led for two laps, opted for Goodyear rain tires at one stage and the decision proved costly in the end, dropping him to a fourth place finish. Christian Fittipaldi, a contender all day, took down third place but teammate Michael Andretti's victory string came to a halt at two.

An ignition problem on the first lap was cured in the pits but cost him a lap and accounted for his 11th place finish. Points leader Jimmy Vasser, the third fastest qualifier, had even poorer luck. Running as high as second in the early going, he was caught out by the rain, executed a rare spin, and ended up just out of the points. Parker Johnstone and Bobby Rahal each had a good day at the track, notching fifth and sixth place respectively. Scott Pruett's handsome outside front row qualifying position went for naught when he was victimized by handling problems.

The top three PPG Cup points positions remained unchanged, Jimmy Vasser 98, Al Unser Jr. 87, and Michael Andretti 73.

Motorsports Marketing at a Championship Level

Kash n' Karry Florida Grand Prix of St. Petersburg
February 21 - 23, 1997
IndyCarnival Australia
April 3 - 6, 1997
ITT Automotive Detroit Grand Prix
June 6 - 8, 1997
Medic Drug Grand Prix of Cleveland
July 11 - 13, 1997

IMG *Motorsports One Erieview Plaza, Suite 1300, Cleveland, Ohio, 44114 (216) 522-1200*

PPG Indy Car World Series Race 10
Medic Drug Grand Prix of Cleveland
Burke Lakefront Airport
Cleveland, Ohio
June 30, 1996
90 Laps, 2.369 Mile Road Course

GIL DE FERRAN NOTCHES VICTORY IN CLEVELAND

This time he made it stick. Gil de Ferran had the '95 Medic Drug Grand Prix of Cleveland virtually in his pocket, but let it slip away by tangling with Scott Pruett after lead-ing 67 laps. This time he was not as dominant, but a lot smarter, stretching out his fuel supply while his competition prayed for him to pit. Second fastest qualifier and eventual runner-up Alex Zanardi did more than pray. He actually got by de Ferran just before the end, only to be repassed by de Ferran on the same lap. Zanardi never got a second chance. Rookie Greg Moore upped his stock with a third place finish from a strong fourth place qualifying spot. Polesitter Jimmy Vasser had another tough day at the office, finishing a lap down in tenth place and losing ground in the PPG Cup points chase. His once substantial margin over Al Unser Jr. dwindled to only three (102 versus 99) with de Ferran coming on strong with a point total of 92. Marlboro Team Penske's Paul Tracy got off to a great start, moving up to third on the first lap from eighth place on the starting grid, but handling problems demoted him back to eighth spot at the end. Texaco-Havoline driver Michael Andretti had a sensational race going, charging into the lead on lap 56 after starting way back in 13th place. Driveline failure sidelined him with nine laps to go and put a big dent in his title campaign. Remarkably, there was only one yellow flag, brought out by a collision involving Parker Johnstone and Eddie Lawson, which sidelined both. The low number of incidents con-tributed to the high winning average speed of 133.736 mph.

AXE

Toronto

Steve Swope

PPG Indy Car World Series Race 11
Molson Indy Toronto
Toronto Exhibition Place
Toronto, Ontario, Canada
July 14, 1996
95 Laps, 1.8 Mile Road Course

ADRIAN FERNANDEZ GETS HIS FIRST INDYCAR VICTORY IN TRAGEDY-TINGED TORONTO

Adrian Fernandez's victory in the Tecate/Quaker State Lola Honda, his first in a four year career, should have occasioned an all out celebration by his Tasman Racing team. Instead, the mood of the entire IndyCar community was subdued. Only three laps from the end of the race, popular rookie driver Jeff Krosnoff was involved in a violent multi-car accident along with Stefan Johansson and polesitter Andre Ribeiro. Krosnoff's car went airborne and hit the barrier. Krosnoff and course worker Gary Avrin died in the incident. Course worker Barbara Johnson was injured. The multi-car accident covered the track with debris and caused the race to be shortened by two laps.

Just before the accident, Fernandez had been gearing up to defend his lead from a pack headed by Alex Zanardi, Bobby Rahal, and Greg Moore on a restart. The restart resulted from a caution period triggered by Michael Andretti's car. Stopped on the course, it represented one more bad luck chapter in Andretti's 1996 book. Under caution for the last two laps completed, his pursuers had no chance to get around Fernandez and finished in the same order. Points leader Jimmy Vasser had a less than happy day, taking down eighth place, still on the lead lap. Closest PPG Cup points producer Al Unser Jr. had an even unhappier one, finishing outside the points, but ahead of third place points producer Gil de Ferran, mired in 18th place. At the end of a downcast day, the leaders on the PPG Cup points board were Vasser 107, Unser 99, and de Ferran 92.

PPG Indy Car World Series Race 12
Marlboro 500
Michigan International Speedway
Brooklyn, Michigan
July 28, 1996
250 Laps, 2 Mile Oval

ANDRE RIBEIRO MASTERS THE MARLBORO 500 AT MICHIGAN

The day started badly for Andre Ribeiro but ended on a high note, center stage on the winner's podium of the Marlboro 500 at Michigan International Speedway. First, the dashing Brazilian was forced to lock up his brakes to avoid an accident on the first green flag lap. This unwelcome incident flat-spotted his tires, calling for an unscheduled pit stop. If this weren't enough bad news, he was nabbed for incorrectly blending into the field following his pit stop.

This double delay sent him to the rear of the field and triggered a torrent of torrid Portuguese inside his cockpit.

Despite the setback he managed to get back into the top five inside of 31 laps, in position to make a move when the front runners run into misfortune, a regular scenario at Michigan. Another Brazilian driver, IndyCar legend Emerson Fittipaldi was a principal, along with Greg Moore, in the opening lap incident which ended up demoting Ribeiro to the back of the pack. Moore was able to continue and actually got in to the lead twice for a total of 31 laps. Fittipaldi did not escape so lightly. Serious, but not life threatening injuries sent him to the hospital and were expected to involve corrective surgery.

Polesitter Jimmy Vasser led the first 15 laps but was destined not to repeat his earlier Michigan victory in the U.S. 500. Indeed, he never got back in front and finished tenth.

Teammate Alex Zanardi took over the point position, exchanging it regularly with Moore and Michael Andretti, keeping the fans on their feet through lap 127 of the 250 scheduled.

Then the anticipated attrition started. Zanardi hit the wall, giving Ribeiro his first taste of the lead, a long stint through lap 210. At this point, Scott Pruett put in a strong bid, leading twice. Pruett's bid ended on lap 235 when his engine expired. The last 15 laps were all Ribeiro, although a fast closing Bryan Herta chased him to the checker. Mauricio Gugelmin, who managed three laps in the lead, finished third. Though a lap in arrears, Al Unser Jr. scored fourth place. The PPG Cup points battle was now extremely tight at the top. Vasser, 112, Unser Jr., 111, and de Ferran, 92. Ribeiro proved that he can shoulder misfortune, earned his second victory of the year, making it two in a row for Tasman Motorsports on top of Fernandez's win in Toronto.

Michael C. Brown

Steve Mohlenkamp

PPG Indy Car World Series Race 13
Miller 200
Mid-Ohio Sports Car Course
Lexington, Ohio
August 11, 1996
83 Laps, 2.25 Mile Road Course

ZANARDI ZIPS AT MID-OHIO WINS MILLER 200 FROM THE POLE

Alex Zanardi likes to win races the simple way; get on the pole, get out in front and stay there til the checkered flag flaps for you. For the second time this season (Portland was the first.) he did just that, losing the lead only to his Target/Ganassi teammate Jimmy Vasser for a total of four laps on pit stops. Vasser was a close second. His 16 PPG Cup points provided a more comfortable 17 point cushion over closest pursuer in the title chase, Al Unser Jr., than the single point separating them after the last race. Unser was involved in a tangle with Parker Johnstone and left Mid-Ohio with no points to show for his efforts. Polesitter Zanardi, more fortunate, left with a $60,000 Marlboro roll over bonus which coupled with today's standard $10,000 Marlboro pole award, brought his season's take to $145,000. Michael Andretti, the fourth fastest qualifier, pressed Vasser consistently but was never positioned to make a clean pass. Bryan Herta, the Shell standard bearer, continuing his string of strong outings, finished fourth, just ahead of teammate and car owner Bobby Rahal, the Miller-backed driver. Not only did Zanardi own the day, he vaulted into the top three in PPG Cup points with a total of 94 behind Vasser with 128 and Unser with 111. The race saw the IndyCar debut of two more Formula One drivers; Jan Magnussen, subbing for an injured Paul Tracy, and Max Papis, taking the vacant seat at Arciero Wells Racing. Both enjoyed their rides, both demonstrated talent. Neither figured prominently in the results.

PPG Indy Car World Series Race 14
Texaco-Havoline 200
Road America
Elkhart Lake, Wisconsin
August 18, 1996
50 Laps, 4 Mile Road Course

WINNER ANDRETTI GETS A BIG BREAK AT ROAD AMERICA

It was a gift from arch rival Al Unser Jr., but Michael Andretti wasn't handing it back. He knew exactly how race leader Unser felt when his Penske Mercedes blew up on the last lap of the Texaco-Havoline 200, dropping the victory into Andretti's lap. Andretti ran out of fuel in almost the same place back in 1989. The misfortune was doubly bitter for Unser, who led half of the event's 58 laps, including 12 of the last 13, and was only a mile away from the checker. Bobby Rahal was another beneficiary of Unser's misfortune picking up second place, his best result of the year, even though slowed by an extra pit stop. Polesitter Alex Zanardi took down the third podium spot, continued to hold third place in the PPG Cup points chase with 109. Jimmy Vasser had an unspectacular day but padded his point total to 136 by finishing sixth. Unser, although immobile, salvaged the tenth finishing position giving him a total of 115. Christian Fittipaldi had a spectacular day going, charging into the lead on the first lap from the second row but lost out to engine failure 43 laps later. Italian rookie Max Papis displayed speed and flair, moving his Toyota powered MCI Reynard into the ninth finishing slot from a way back qualifying position. Juan Manuel Fangio brought his Toyota powered Eagle home in eighth place, also from far back. Not a bad day for proponents of the new powerplant. Parker Johnstone and Davy Jones escaped unharmed from flips, Johnstone's due to a tangle with Paul Tracy, back in action after recovering from a practice accident at Michigan.

Paul Webb

Steve Swope

PPG Indy Car World Series Race 15
Molson Indy Vancouver
Concord Pacific Place
Vancouver, B.C., Canada
September 1, 1996
100 Laps, 1.703 Mile Road Course

VICTORY AT VANCOUVER GOES TO MICHAEL ANDRETTI

Victory in Vancouver's Molson Indy, his fifth of the year, vaulted Michael Andretti into the thick of the PPG Cup title chase and made him the winningest driver of '96. Only the Kmart/Texaco-Havoline driver and record setting polesitter Alex Zanardi, were truly in the hunt for top honors. Zanardi rocketed off the start line, led the first 18 laps handily. His chances for a third win of the year vaporized when he tangled with P.J. Jones in a failed passing attempt. This misfortune handed the lead to Andretti, who drove flawlessly to the finish, out in front and flying. Bobby Rahal had another good day at the office posting his second runner-up finish in a row, after qualifying third fastest. He admitted that he was never properly positioned to make a clean passing run on Andretti. Christian Fittipaldi, the Kmart/Budweiser standard bearer, became the second Newman-Haas driver on the podium taking down third place. Gil de Ferran just missed the podium, finishing fourth, with Al Unser Jr. just astern, at the checker. Jimmy Vasser had another, "hang in there," seventh place finish. As the PPG Cup scoreboard read at day's end, Vasser, 142, Andretti, 128, and Unser, 125 were the only three with theoretical chances at the PPG Cup to be decided at Laguna Seca next weekend. While Zanardi's failed passing gamble took him out of contention for top PPG Cup honors, he did secure a handsome consolation prize. When chief rival for Rookie of the Year honors, Greg Moore, failed to finish, Zanardi wrapped up this this title and its $50,000 honorarium.

PPG Indy Car World Series Race 16
Toyota Grand Prix of Monterey
Laguna Seca Raceway
Monterey, California
September 8, 1996
83 Laps, 2.238 Mile Road Course

CHIP GANASSI'S TARGET TWOSOME CAPTURES LAGUNA SECA

Alex Zanardi's Daring Pass Takes Toyota Grand Prix of Monterey

Jimmy Vasser Earns the $1 Million PPG Cup as Challengers Fade

What a day for Target/Ganassi Racing. First, rookie Alex Zanardi "stole" the race with a daring, almost incredible last lap pass of

Bryan Herta. Next, teammate Jimmy Vasser, needing only sixth place to win the 1996 PPG Cup, flashed across the finish line a solid fourth, good for a point total of 154 and the '96 PPG Cup, triggering a celebration to be remembered in the annals of IndyCar racing. Zanardi's spectacular win earned him a tie with Michael Andretti for second place PPG Cup honors at 128 points. The tie was decided in Andretti's favor on the basis of his five victories to Zanardi's three. Neither Michael Andretti nor Al Unser Jr., who might have been able to pressure Vasser in the title countdown, were in the hunt today. Andretti had tire problems after minor contact with Bobby Rahal, finished ninth. Unser, off the pace, had to settle for 16th. Scott Pruett edged past Vasser for the third podium placement. Except for a single lap led by Vasser on pit stops, Zanardi

and Herta owned the race; polesitter Zanardi the first half; second fastest qualifier Herta the second half (except of course, for that critical last lap). Zanardi's daring do earned him a $45,000 Marlboro Pole Award bonus. Each registered 41 laps out in front. Vasser demonstrated not only speed in his winning campaign; four victories, four poles, but consistency; scoring points in 15 out of 16 races. He deserved the recogntion accorded him as a worthy champion. Piling up a big lead early, at one point, late in the season, he was only a single point ahead. Going into the final race he could have been caught by the two biggest names in the trade, but never faltered. On the mechanical side, the Reynard/Honda/Firestone combination demonstrated, at the end of the season as it had at the beginning, that it was the winning package of '96.

Steve Swope

IRL's First Year Produces Co-Champions, Buzz Calkins & Scott Sharp

Just as its head, Tony George, promised, the new Indy Racing League opened on schedule at the beautiful new Walt Disney World one mile oval on January 27, 1996. George wisely brought on board veteran Formula One and Indy car race organizer Jack Long to help get the opening event off the ground. Long stayed throughout the first year until ex-Goodyear racing head Leo Mehl, a recognized dean of the motorsports world, accepted the no. 2 post in the organization on a permanent basis.

At Disney, there was a sellout inaugural crowd of 51,000. They watched 20 drivers, ranging from veterans Arie Luyendyk, Roberto Guerrero and Scott Brayton to outright rookies up from the lesser oval track series, take the starter's flag.

Buddy Lazier, an under-appreciated Indy Car veteran, took the pole and led the first 28 laps in a '95 Reynard Ford, lost out to brake problems. Star rookie Tony Stewart then assumed the lead but the whole second half belonged to Calkins. So did the handsome $122,500 winner's payout. Detroit's Robbie Buhl was third. The IRL was now launched, off the starting grid and into the record books. On to Phoenix for round two, where experience paid off. Arie Luyendyk set a new record in qualifying and came home on top. 22 cars started. Scott Sharp and Mike Groff, also veterans, followed Luyendyk to the checker. With the opening rounds completed, the focus was on the Indianapolis 500, the centerpiece and raison d'etre for the IRL.

With the rival CART group boycotting the world's biggest single day sporting event despite its rich tradition and equally rich rewards, there were still 77 entries. As an indication of the caliber of the event the qualifying record was broken by Arie Luyendyk at 237.498 mph, too late, however, to gain the pole. That went to Scott Brayton, again. The much admired Brayton later lost his life in a practice accident for the race he loved.

On race day, before huge crowds, as usual, star rookie Tony Stewart jumped into the lead but capitulated to engine problems after only 82 laps. The race evolved into a duel between veterans Buddy Lazier and Davy Jones. Lazier prevailed, all the more remarkably, since he was driving with a broken back incurred in an accident at Phoenix. The record for the race's fastest lap was broken by Stewart at 236.103 mph. The race payout at $8,114,600 was a record. Lazier's take of $1,367,854 was just short of Al Unser Jr.'s $1,373,813 in 1994. The race was won on Firestone tires, breaking a long Goodyear string. Officially, the Indy Racing League's first season had ended, the original objective being to cap the season with the Indy 500. Since no tie breaker system was in place, Buzz Calkins and Scott Sharp were declared co-champions. Each got $31,000 from the $500,000 point fund. A separate $500,000 entrant's fund listed A.J. Foyt Enterprises at $32,000 and Bradley Motorsports at $30,000, the top beneficiaries.

The 1996 calendar still had two events scheduled, at New Hampshire and Las Vegas. The Indy Racing League wisely moved to a calendar year championship for 1997 and counted these two as part of the new season. Scott Sharp won his first Indy car race at New Hampshire, as did Richie Hearn at the handsome new Las Vegas venue. Indy Racing League had its first year in the record book, had achieved its goals of developing new American drivers and showcasing oval track events.

IRL's sophomore year of 1997 will be a whole new undertaking. The new sanctioning group inaugurates its own formula for cars; designed to be slower, less expensive and safer. The same for engines, normally aspirated 4-liter overhead cam stock blocks, also expected to be slightly less powerful and cheaper. Oldsmobile and Nissan have stepped up to the bat on the engine front; Dallara and G Force on the chassis side. Both engine manufacturers have considerable experience, from their IMSA sportscar involvement, with racing V8s based on their stock production engines. Oldsmobile would dearly love to win the 1997 Indiana-polis 500, which coincides with the division's 100th anniversary. Olds got off to a head start in race testing their engines, which indeed were down on power from the turbocharged powerplants in use in 1996 but putting out sufficient horsepower to provide exciting racing. The new chassis are expected to be, if anything, stiffer than their predecessors. Realistically the Indy Racing League's 1996 season could be considered a dress rehearsal for '97 when the new sanctioning group performs with the new equipment that was a key component in their master plan.

Long term CART and Indy 500 sponsor PPG Industries has exhibited its confidence by posting substantial awards for drivers in the new series. With the Indianapolis 500 firmly in their "league," the Indy Racing League has a powerful feature attraction and seems poised to tackle its sophomore year with confidence. One thing for sure, every car you see will be a brand new '97 model. The new racers will debut at Walt Disney World in early 1997.

Bob Straus

Indy Racing League Race 1
Indy 200 at Walt Disney World
Presented by Aurora
Walt Disney World Speedway
Orlando, Florida
January 27, 1996
200 Laps, 1 Mile Oval

BUZZ CALKINS MAKES HISTORY AS WINNER OF IRL INAUGURAL

Buzz Calkins will go into the record books with several firsts. First driver to win an Indy Racing League event, first driver to win on the hand-some new one mile layout at Walt Disney World Speedway. Calkins started fifth behind polesitter Buddy Lazier who led the first 28 laps before giving way up front to ex-USAC standout Tony Stewart who led the pack for the next 36 laps. Stewart eventually lost out to sus-pension failure. Calkins got his first taste of leadership on lap 66 before Stan Wattles, Robbie Buhl, and Davey Hamilton each enjoyed short stints in front. On lap 76, Calkins took over again, this time for good. IRL entrant and protagonist A.J. Foyt was tagged by misfortune. Two of his entries went out via the accident route, Davey Hamilton on his own,

Sharp in a tangle with Eddie Cheever. Calkins' closest pursuer was Stewart, whose late race charge fell short by .866 seconds. Attendance stood at a sellout 51,000. Of particular interest was the husky purse of $1,078,500, $122,500 of which went to Calkins. Third place Robbie Buhl took down $87,250.

IRL founder Tony George could afford the luxury of a smile, knowing that his creation had met its first test, that of organizing, and completing an inaugural race on a new oval. The new American drivers he wants to help, today upstaged the veterans, Roberto Guerrero, Arie Luyendyk, Scott Brayton, and Eddie Cheever.

Indy Racing League Race 2
Phoenix 200
Phoenix International Raceway
Phoenix, Arizona
March 24, 1996
200 Laps, 1 Mile Oval

SCORE ONE FOR THE VETERANS ARIE LUYENDYK TAKES PHOENIX

Phoenix, the site of the IRL's second race and Walt Disney World, the site of its first, have oval tracks exactly the same one mile length. Any similarities in the two contests stop there. Humbled in the opener, veteran drivers, led by pole-sitter Arie Luyendyk, took down all three of the top spots. The 1990 Indianapolis 500 winner, who still holds the race record (average speed 185.981 mph) there, had a comfortable 8.896 second cushion over runner-up Scott Sharp at the end. Sharp, who led 40 laps, was one of three A.J. Foyt entries. Teammate Mike Groff took down third place, while Davey Hamilton suffered electrical problems before the halfway mark. Luyendyk led 122 of the 200 laps contested, was never under pressure during the final third of the event. Robbie Buhl, Tony Stewart and Richie Hearn all enjoyed brief stints in front of the pack. Hearn, who shared the front row at the start with Luyendyk, finished fourth, the other two were victims of mechanical failure. With two races in the record book, the eyes of the IRL were clearly focused on the month of May in Indianapolis where the monetary rewards for success would dwarf today's generous $132,000 payout to winner Luyendyk.

Ron McQueeney/IMS Photo

Indy Racing League Race 3
Indianapolis 500
Indianapolis Motor Speedway
Indianapolis, Indiana
May 26, 1996
200 Laps, 2.5 Mile Oval

BROKEN BACK CAN'T STOP BUDDY LAZIER HE TAKES THE 80th INDIANAPOLIS 500

Buddy Lazier overcame constant pain and the best that Davy Jones could throw at him in the final countdown, to capture the richest Indianapolis 500 in history. Lazier took down $1,367,854 from the 500's biggest ever purse at $8,114,600. Jones' consolation prize for runner-up honors was a hefty $632,503. Rookie Richie Hearn got $375,203 for his third place effort. There were records set on the track, too. Eddie Cheever posted the fastest race lap at 236.103 mph. The race's Rookie of the Year, Tony Stewart, posted the fastest ever leading lap at 232.412. It was one of the 31 he led from the pole, the most for any rookie in the race's history. Stewart suffered engine failure after 82 laps, Cheever held on for an 11th place finish. Lazier had a taste of the lead on three earlier occasions. Alessandro Zampedri, running a strong race, was credited with fourth place despite his last lap tangle with Roberto Guerrero and Eliseo Salazar. The latter pair finished fifth and sixth. The race's key chapter was Lazier's pass of Davy Jones on lap 193 and his ability to stave off Jones' attempts to repass on the last lap restart. Lazier admitted after the race that, "It hasn't sunk in yet." The rewards attending the biggest day in his 26 year old life might take him a while to get used to but he was determined to enjoy them all the way.

Another record set was the 236.986 mph average for Arie Luyendyk's qualifying run, too late to take the pole, which went to Scott Brayton for the second year in a row. Sadly Brayton died in a post-qualifying practice crash. Long missing from the Speedway, Danny Ongais took over the car qualified by Brayton and managed to finish seventh despite a spin. Luyendyk completed only 149 of the 200 scheduled laps.

80th Indianapolis 500

FIN. POS.	ST. POS.	CAR NO.	DRIVER	CAR NAME	LAPS	STATUS	AWARDS
1	5	91	BUDDY LAZIER	Hemelgarn/Delta Faucet/Montana	200	Running	$1,367,854
2	2	70	DAVY JONES	Delco Electronics High Tech Team Galles	200	Running	632,503
3	15	4	RICHIE HEARN*	Della Penna/Ralph's/Fuji Film	200	Running	375,203
4	7	8	ALESSANDRO ZAMPEDRI	Mi-Jack/AGIP/Xcel	199	Accident	270,853
5	6	21	ROBERTO GUERRERO	WavePhore/Pennzoil	198	Accident	315,503
6	3	7	ELISEO SALAZAR	Cristal/Copect Mobil	197	Accident	226,653
7	33	32	DANNY ONGAIS#	Glidden Menards Special	197	Running	228,253
8	30	52	HIDESHI MATSUDA	Team Taisan/Beck Motorsports	197	Running	233,953
9	23	54	ROBBIE BUHL	Original Coors/Beck Motorsports	197	Running	195,403
10	21	11	SCOTT SHARP	Conseco AJ Foyt Racing	194	Accident	202,053
11	4	3	EDDIE CHEEVER	Quaker State Menards Special	189	Running	206,103
12	10	14	DAVEY HAMILTON*	AJ Foyt Copenhagen	181	Running	184,003
13	8	22	MICHEL JOURDAIN JR.*	Herdez Quaker State Viva Mexico!	177	Running	193,653
14	18	45	LYN ST. JAMES	Spirit of San Antonio	153	Accident	182,603
15	32	44	SCOTT HARRINGTON*	Gold Eagle/Mech. Laundry/Harrington	150	Accident	190,753
16	20	5	ARIE LUYENDYK	Byrd's Cafeteria/Bryant Htg & Cooling	149	Accident	216,503
17	9	12	BUZZ CALKINS*	Bradley Food Marts/Hoosier Lottery	148	Brakes	173,553
18	19	27	JIM GUTHRIE*	Team Blueprint	144	Engine	168,453
19	14	30	MARK DISMORE*	Quaker State Menards Special	129	Engine	161,253
20	11	60	MIKE GROFF	Valvoline Cummins Craftsman Special	122	Fire	158,503
21	28	34	FERMIN VELEZ*	Scandia/Xcel/Royal Purple	107	Fire	176,653
22	31	43	JOE GOSEK*	Scandia/Fanatics Only/Xcel	106	Radiator	169,653
23	26	10	BRAD MURPHEY*	Hemelgarn Delta Faucet/Firestone	91	Suspension	177,853
24	1	20	TONY STEWART*	Menards/Glidden/Quaker State	82	Engine	222,053
25	25	90	RACIN GARDNER*	Scandia/Slick Gardner Enterprises	76	Suspension	149,853
26	22	41	MARCO GRECO	AJ Foyt Enterprises	64	Engine	153,303
27	13	9	STEPHAN GREGOIRE	Hemelgarn/Delta Faucet/Firestone	59	Fire	147,103
28	27	16	JOHNNY PARSONS	Team Blueprint	48	Radiator	161,203
29	29	75	JOHNNY O'CONNELL*	Mech. Laundry/Cunningham/Firestone	47	Fuel Pickup	145,553
30	12	33	MICHELE ALBORETO*	Rio Hotel & Cas./Perry Ellis/Royal Purple	43	Gear Box	144,953
31	17	18	JOHN PAUL JR.	V-Line/Earl's/ Crowne Plaza/Keco	10	Ignition	144,203
32	24	96	PAUL DURANT*	Manaras/Simu/Glenmark/Miller Eads	9	Engine	149,153
33	16	64	JOHNNY UNSER*	Ruger-Titanium/Project Indy	0	Transmiss.	143,953

*Rookie
- 5/19 named to drive car qualified by Scott Brayton
TIME OF RACE: 3 hours 22 minutes 45.753 seconds
AVERAGE SPEED: 147.956 mph
MARGIN OF VICTORY: 0.695 second
CAUTION FLAGS: 10 for 49 laps

LAP LEADERS:
Tony Stewart: 1-31, 42-54
Roberto Guerrero: 32-37, 55-70
Buddy Lazier: 38-41, 121-133, 193-200
Davy Jones: 71-86, 98-120, 159-160, 168-169
Alessandro Zampedri: 170-189

Indy Racing League Race 4*
True Value 200
New Hampshire Int. Speedway
August 18, 1996
200 Laps, 1 Mile Oval

SCOTT SHARP WINS ONE FOR A.J., NEW HAMPSHIRE IS FOYT'S FIRST VICTORY AS A TEAM OWNER

A.J. Foyt is a living legend as an Indy car driver. His record as a car owner since stepping out of the cockpit is a little less spectacular. Young Scott Sharp finally made him a winner at New Hampshire. It was Sharp's first Indy car victory too, which doubled the reasons to celebrate. Tony Stewart's luck continued to be incredibly bad. By mid-race he had a full lap lead over polesitter Richie Hearn, in second place at this juncture. Arie Luyendyk and Sharp were even further behind, running third and fourth. Lap 123 produced a rain induced delay of 45 minutes. When action resumed, Stewart quickly put the field at a two lap disadvantage. Luyendyk and Hearn both by now had mechanical problems, so that Sharp moved up to the second slot. This time it wasn't engine problems that caused Stewart's downfall. He suffered an electrical malfunction on lap 182. Sharp inherited the lead and cruised to victory circle by 20.4 seconds over Calkins, with ex-Formula One driver Michele Alboreto taking down third place. With Stewart gone, Sharp's only real concern was fuel, but he was able to nurse his Lola Ford to the finish line in front.

Dan Bianchi

*4th race of the '96 calendar year will count as the first of IRL's '97 championship year.

Indy Racing League Race 5*
Las Vegas 500K
Las Vegas Motor Speedway
Las Vegas, Nevada
September 15, 1996
200 Laps, 1.5 Mile Oval

RICHIE HEARN AVOIDS THE ACCIDENTS, WINS LAS VEGAS INAUGURAL

The new Las Vegas Motor Speedway is a handsome, state of the art new facility but proved to be a handful for drivers facing it for the first time. The major problem had nothing to do with the track's layout or construction. High winds and swirling sand were believed to be the villains behind eight accidents, resulting in 83 laps under caution. Even such an experienced veteran as Arie Luyendyk managed to find the wall. None of these distractions bothered Richie Hearn, who started eighth and first took the lead at the halfway mark. Johnny O'Connell and Robby Gordon provided the stiffest opposition for Hearn, but Gordon ran into wheel-bearing problems and O'Connell ran into the wall. Surprise runner-up was Mexico's Michel Jourdain Jr. who started back in 22nd place and was 1.693 seconds behind at the end. Veteran Mike Groff took down third place. Las Vegas proved, as expected, to be blisteringly fast but Hearn found his way around it and notched his first win of the '97 IRL season, three months early. In the IRL's five races to date, there have been five different winners.

*5th race of the '96 calendar year will count as the second of IRL's '97 championship year.

Ron McQueeney/IMS Photo

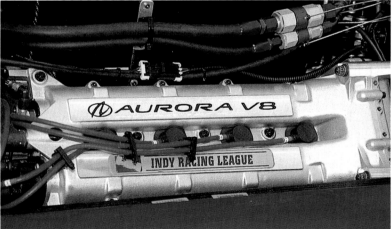

Dan Bianchi

New Look for Indy Racing League

Ron McQueeney/IMS Photo

New chassis by G Force and Dallara, designed to produce less downforce and be safer, as well as cheaper, powered by new stock block engines (Aurora and Infinity are the first suppliers) are the rule for Indy Racing League competitors in 1997. The engines are 4-liter, 4-cam all alloy V-8s developed from stock blocks. Slightly less powerful than the turbocharged pure racing 2.65-liter engines used by the Indy Racing League in '96, (and still in use on the rival CART circuit), the new V-8s are designed to reduce speed and lower costs at no sacrifice in the level of competition. Shown at top, the G Force Aurora favored by Eddie Cheever, now a team owner as well as a driver. The Aurora and Infinity engines get a close-up, left.

1 Co-Champion... **Buzz Calkins** went into the record books as the first ever winner of an Indy Racing League race - and its first Co-Champion.

Walt Kuhn/IMS Photo

Dan Bianchi

1 Foyt Protege... **Scott Sharp** won his first IRL race after the official '96 season was over, piled up regular season points for a co-championship.

Dan Bianchi

3 Consistent Campaigner... **Robbie Buhl** took down the third highest point total in the IRL's abbreviated first season.

Dan Bianchi

4 Las Vegas Winner... **Richie Hearn** skirted the accidents in the Las Vegas inaugural, scored his first IRL victory.

Dan Bianchi

5 Still Speedy... **Roberto Guerrero** retains his high speed skills - and his lack of luck.

Dan Bianchi

6 Steady Veteran... **Mike Groff** used his experience to advantage to score a pair of third places.

Geoffrey Hewitt

7 Speedway Flyer... **Arie Luyendyk** nailed down the victory at Phoenix, was the fastest qualifier for the Indianapolis 500, but failed to finish.

8 Fast But Unfortunate... **Tony Stewart** had no trouble taking the lead. Holding it in the face of mechanical problems was another story.

Dan Bianchi

Dan Bianchi

9 Another Foyt Protege... **Davey Hamilton** showed potential.

Dan Bianchi

10 Road Racing Champion... **Johnny O'Connell** adapted quickly to ovals, but was involved in a major shunt at Las Vegas.

Most Versatile of '96... Scott Sharp, shown with Rain-X's Dave Ohlhausen, won a race in the Indy Racing League, two in IMSA's Exxon World Sportscar series, just missed in the Trans-Am Championship.

Bob Steig

Back-to-Back Titles for Ford's Tommy Kendall in the Trans-Am Championship

Geoffrey Hewitt

On the '96 Trans-Am Tour, each of the top three drivers, Mustang mounted Tommy Kendall and Dorsey Schroeder, and Ron Fellows, aboard a Camaro, scored four victories. Only two other drivers, both Chevrolet protagonists, Jamie Galles and Paul Gentilozzi were able to get into the win column. The "tie breaker" which earned Kendall his second title in a row was the five point bonus for fastest qualifiers, awarded as part of Trans-Am's inverted start system for the fastest five qualifiers. Kendall, quick as ever, was the top qualifier eight times to twice for Schroeder and Fellows. Boris Said III and Jamie Galles, were the only other fastest qualifiers. Kendall also proved more capable at overcoming his handicap when starting fifth, as required when he captured qualifying honors. Fellows, in pursuit of the Trans-Am Championship he has never won despite being achingly close, started the season in fine form. He won the season opener at St. Petersburg in the new Sunoco Camaro. Arch rival Kendall, in the All Sport Mustang, dropped out, not a great start for a title defense. Kendall, however, bounced back in the second round at Homestead. Next, young Jamie Galles collected his first ever Trans-Am win at Long Beach aboard the

ICI/Glidden Camaro. Phoenix was Schroeder's turn in victory circle, in the Raybestos Mustang. Paul Gentilozzi became the fifth driver to win in the first five races when the Trans-Am Tour ventured northward to Canada's Mosport circuit.

From this point on, Kendall, Schroeder, and Fellows were the only drivers to win. Schroeder's love affair with the Lime Rock circuit stayed in bloom. He added a third victory to his two previous wins at the Connecticut road course, giving him a sweep of every Trans-Am event there that he has entered. Schroeder next "owned" the Motor City 100 in Detroit, the "Automotive Capitol of the World," gaining bragging rights for Ford. Kendall did much the same in Cleveland, where Rain-X backed Greg Pickett scored well earned runner-up honors, his second of the season. The winner's circle at the Minneapolis race was annexed by Kendall, putting him up front by a single point in the season long tussle with Schroeder. Fellows won as the Tour revisited Canada for the Trois-Rivieres event and Schroeder regained the points lead. Schroeder padded his lead to 11 points with the win at Watkins Glen, after a race long battle with Kendall. In the Road America outing, Kendall teammate

Boris Said III had the early lead, graciously handed it, the win and some key points to Kendall. Fellows took the last two races of the year at Dallas and the exciting new Reno course, but to no avail in his title bid. He did secure third place in the season's points totals. Adding to Fellows' disappointment was Chevrolet's mid-season announcement that they would no longer support the series at the factory level. Schroeder failed to finish at Dallas, leaving Kendall in firm command of the championship chase as he ran out his second title in a row. Kendall's eight quickest qualifying runs, 743 laps led, and six fastest race laps topped the statistics. Ford gained the '96 Manufacturers' Championship.

R.J. Valentine, the sportsman-businessman driver with Pennzoil backing, capped his career by winning the Optima Batteries Quick Charger Award with a daring dash from last to 11th at Reno.

John Miller IV annexed Rookie of the Year honors while Max Lagod was named Raybestos Rising Star of the Year. Despite Chevrolet's departure it's likely that Trans-Am will remain a Mustang-Camaro face off in '97. However, Buzz McCall, Fellows' car owner, indicated that he did not intend to return.

Dan Bianchi

1 Champion Again... **Tommy Kendall** earned his second Trans-Am Championship title in a row by outqualifying everybody else - and winning four races. (378 Trans-Am points)

Dan Bianchi

2 Chief Challenger... **Dorsey Schroeder** matched Kendall in the win column with four, but lost out on qualifying bonus points. (348 Trans-Am points)

Dan Bianchi

3 Foiled Flyer... **Ron Fellows** won as many races as the top two, lost out to mechanical problems. (284 Trans-Am points)

Dan Bianchi

4 First Time Winner... **Jamie Galles** scored at Long Beach, hounded the top three all year. (274 Trans-Am points)

Bob Steig

Dan Bianchi

5 Former Champion... **Scott Sharp** missed two Trans-Am events to run IRL Indy car races, still managed to make the top five. (263 Trans-Am points)

Dan Bianchi

6 Team Player... **Boris Said III** proved to be a fast and worthy Kendall teammate, conceded the lead in a critical race to Tommy. (245 Trans-Am points)

Dan Bianchi

7 Front Runner... **Brian Simo** scored no victories, but regularly ran with the leaders. (243 Trans-Am points)

Dan Bianchi

8 Very Fast Veteran... **Greg Pickett** just missed victory circle on two occasions.
(240 Trans-Am points)

Dan Bianchi

9 Dual Role... **Bill Saunders** combined team ownership with driving, performed well at both. (230 Trans-Am points)

Dan Bianchi

10 Aided By Experience... **Jon Gooding** came to the series with speed, benefited from additional experience. (213 Trans-Am points)

11 Mosport Master... **Paul Gentilozzi** was one of only two drivers outside of the top three to win a race. (200 Trans-Am points)

Dan Bianchi

Dan Bianchi

12 **R.J. Valentine**, regularly one ot the top performing owner/drivers, made the top dozen in the points parade. (198 Trans-Am points)

Trans-Am Championship
1996 Drivers' Points Standings

POS.	DRIVER	CAR	POINTS	PURSE
1	TOM KENDALL	Mustang Cobra	378	$253,700
2	DORSEY SCHROEDER	Mustang Cobra	348	226,100
3	RON FELLOWS	Chevrolet Camaro	284	122,775
4	JAMIE GALLES	Chevrolet Camaro	274	98,000
5	SCOTT SHARP	Chevrolet Camaro	263	103,200
6	BORIS SAID III	Mustang Cobra	245	102,000
7	BRIAN SIMO	Mustang Cobra	243	78,400
8	GREG PICKETT	Chevrolet Camaro	240	73,775
9	BILL SAUNDERS	Chevrolet Camaro	230	68,900
10	JON GOODING	Mustang Cobra	213	56,700
11	PAUL GENTILOZZI	Chevrolet Camaro	200	81,850
12	R.J. VALENTINE	Chevrolet Camaro	198	58,400
13	JOHN W. MILLER IV	Chevrolet Camaro	147	35,900
14	DALE PHELON	Mustang Cobra	145	35,800
15	MAX LAGOD	Chevrolet Camaro	128	40,500
16	BOB RUMAN	Chevrolet Camaro	122	25,050
17	LEIGHTON REESE	Pontiac Grand Prix	82	14,650
18	DINO CRESCENTINI	Chevrolet Camaro	74	13,050
19	KENNY BUPP	Chevrolet Camaro	63	9,150
20	STEVE HODGE	Chevrolet Camaro	49	7,200
21	DON SAK	Oldsmobile Cutlass	47	12,200
22	BRUCE NESBITT	Mustang Cobra	47	7,400
23	DON MELUZIO	Chevrolet Camaro	44	7,600
24	BILL EAGLE	Chevrolet Camaro	42	5,700
25	JERRY SIMMONS	Chevrolet Camaro	29	9,700
26	RICK DITTMAN	Chevrolet Camaro	36	4,500
27	CRAIG SHAFER	Chevrolet Camaro	34	4,400
28	JIM MAGUIRE	Chevrolet Camaro	30	3,500
29	TOM GLOY	Ford Mustang	25	11,000
30	ERIC VAN DE POELE	Chevrolet Camaro	24	4,450
31	GLENN ANDREW	Chevrolet Camaro	23	3,800
	DOMENIC TOTO	Oldsmobile	22	2,600
33	JOHNNY O'CONNELL	Ford Mustang	21	4,550
34	WAYNE AKERS	Ford Mustang	20	2,800
	PETER SHEA	Chevrolet Camaro	20	2,800
36	JOHN FERGUS	Ford Mustang	19	3,750
37	TRENT TERRY	Oldsmobile Cutlass	19	2,200
38	FRANK CIOPPETTINI JR.	Chevrolet Camaro	18	2,000
39	CHARLES NEARBURG	Ford Mustang	17	2,500
40	RANDY RUHLMAN	Dodge Daytona	17	1,900
41	JIM DERHAAG	Chevrolet Camaro	16	3,300
42	JAMES G. CRIST	Oldsmobile Cutlass	15	2,400
43	WALLY CASTRO	Ford Mustang	15	2,100
44	MARK PIELSTICKER	Chevrolet Camaro	14	2,900
	RAY KONG	Chevrolet Camaro	14	3,400
46	ED HINCHCLIFF	Ford Mustang	13	2,000
47	TED SULLIVAN	Chevrolet Camaro	13	2,100
48	DAVID RUBINS	Chevrolet Camaro	12	1,700
49	KERRY HITT	Chevrolet Corvette	12	2,100
50	JON LEAVY	Chevrolet Camaro	11	1,300

Trans-Am Championship Race 1
Kash n' Karry Grand Prix
of St. Petersburg
St. Petersburg, Florida
February 25, 1996
63 Laps, 110.8 Miles

Trans-Am Championship Race 2
Florida Dodge Dealers 400
Weekend
Homestead, Florida
March 16, 1996
46 Laps, 101.66 Miles

Trans-Am Championship Race 3
Optima Batteries Trans-Am Classic
Long Beach, California
April 14, 1996
58 Laps, 92.22 Miles

RON FELLOWS OPENS TITLE CAMPAIGN WITH ST. PETERSBURG VICTORY

Ron Fellows got off to a good start in his campaign to take the Trans-Am Championship that has eluded him by winning the season opening Kash n' Karry Grand Prix of St. Petersburg in his new Sunoco Camaro. He didn't even have to go head-to-head with his old nemesis Tommy Kendall to notch the win. Kendall posted the fastest qualifying time, an area he would dominate over the season, but fell to mechanical problems after only 14 laps. The same fate fell to teammate Boris Said III, fifth fastest qualifier, who started on the pole. Dorsey Schroeder, in the Raybestos Mustang, produced one of his late race surges but it fell 1.93 seconds short of catching the flying Fellows. Brian Simo notched the third podium position in his Valvoline Mustang. Jamie Galles, in the ICI/Glidden Camaro and Scott Sharp, in the Cytomax Camaro, both capable of making things interesting for Fellows, finished seventh and eighth, respectively, just ahead of R.J. Valentine, up from 15th on the starting grid.

TOMMY KENDALL HUSTLES TO HOMESTEAD WIN

Ace qualifier Tommy Kendall could manage only the fifth fastest qualifying time at the new Homestead circuit, but this translated to the pole position and a front running ride to victory circle. Ron Fellows, who was the fastest qualifier, moved up to third place at the end from his mandated fifth starting position. Paul Gentilozzi, fourth fastest in qualifying had a better day than his DNF in the season opener, gained runner-up honors. He was off Fellows' pace by 1.217 seconds. Jamie Galles again furnished evidence of his race winning potential by placing fourth, ahead of Boris Said III and Scott Sharp in one of Greg Pickett's Rain-X/Cytomax Camaros. R.J. Valentine, in pursuit of the Optima Batteries Quick Charger Award, had to defer to Max Lagod despite moving up five places to ninth place, just astern of Dorsey Schroeder, in the Raybestos Mustang, who would later in the season be a top contender for the title. Kendall's victory helped overcome the disappointment of his DNF in the season opener.

JAMIE GALLES GRABS HIS FIRST TRANS-AM WIN AT LONG BEACH

Talented young driver Jamie Galles wheeled his ICI/Glidden Camaro home first in the Optima Batteries Classic at Long Beach. It was the maiden voyage to the winner's circle for Galles, who is the son of successful car dealer and Indy car team owner, Rick Galles. Tony Ave, on the pole by virtue of his fifth fastest qualifying time, led the first eight laps, was displaced by Dorsey Schroeder. Schroeder was muscled out of the lead by Tommy Kendall, who then led more than half of the race's 58 laps before encountering mechanical problems. He salvaged a seventh place finish. Galles inherited the lead and might have had his hands full holding off a fast closing Scott Sharp, in the Rain-X Oil Energizer Camaro, except for the yellow flag generated by Dale Phelon's crash. The race ended under yellow with Galles 1.196 seconds out in front of Sharp. R.J. Valentine moved up nine places from his 17th starting slot, setting a fast pace in his campaign for the year's Optima Batteries Quick Charger Award.

Trans-Am Championship Race 4
Chevrolet Desert Star Classic
Weekend
Phoenix, Arizona
April 20, 1996
65 Laps, 98.15 Miles

Trans-Am Championship Race 5
The Sunoco Ultra 94
Trans-Am Classic
Mosport Park, Ontario, Canada
May 19, 1996
40 Laps, 98.36 Miles

Trans-Am Championship Race 6
Dodge Dealers
Grand Prix of Lime Rock
Lakeville, Connecticut
May 27, 1996
66 Laps, 100.98 Miles

SCHROEDER SNAPS UP THE VICTORY AT PHOENIX

It was Dorsey Schroeder's turn in the winner's circle. He brought his Raybestos Mustang home on top in the Chevrolet Desert Star Classic by 1.873 seconds over Scott Sharp in the Rain-X Oil Energizer Camaro, the runner-up for the second race in a row. Jamie Galles, in the ICI/Glidden Camaro, the winner last time out, out accelerated Sharp into the lead and as late as lap 49 of the 65 scheduled looked like a winner. After that it was all Sharp and Schroeder, trading the lead three times, with the Mustang driver on top when it counted. Galles ended up in third place. Tommy Kendall and Ron Fellows were both off the pace, finishing sixth and eighth, respectively. This despite Fellows' fastest qualifying time and fastest race lap. Schroeder's win made him a contender for the '96 drivers' title.

GENTILOZZI LEADS EVERY LAP AT MOSPORT

Starting on the pole, Paul Gentilozzi nosed his HighwayMaster Camaro in front in the first lap of the Sunoco Ultra 94 Classic at Mosport and was never headed. Jamie Galles came closest, a mere .349 of a second behind at the finish. Gentilozzi was the fifth different winner in the year's five Trans-Am events to date. Tommy Kendall was the fastest qualifier and posted the fastest race lap, but could move up only two spots, from his fifth position on the starting grid. Kendall's arch rival Ron Fellows had a dismal day, starting second but lasting only nine laps due to mechanical gremlins. Greg Pickett picked up 23 useful points for his fourth place finish in the Rain-X Oil Energizer Camaro, while Dorsey Schroeder, the winner last time out, managed seventh place today.

SCHROEDER SUPREME AT LIME ROCK, AGAIN

When the Trans-Am Championship stops at Lime Rock, watch out for Dorsey Schroeder. In two previous appearances, he was the winner. Today's Dodge Dealers Grand Prix at the beautiful Connecticut hillside circuit was no exception. Nobody was even close at the finish. Second place again went to Greg Pickett's Cytomax/Rain-X Camaro with Tommy Kendall cruising home in the third slot. Ron Fellows took the lead from polesitter Schroeder for the mid-section of the race but fell to differential problems. Nobody else ever got into the lead. Fastest qualifier Boris Said III went out after 52 laps with differential problems. He set the race's fastest lap. R.J. Valentine posted another top ten finish, up six spots from his 13th starting position.

Geoffrey Hewitt

Steve Mohlenkamp

Trans-Am Championship Race 7
Motor City 100
Belle Isle, Detroit, Michigan
June 8, 1996
48 Laps, 100.8 Miles

DORSEY SCHROEDER IN FRONT ALL THE WAY IN DETROIT

Dorsey Schroeder outsprinted polesitter Dale Phelon into the first corner of the Motor City 100 circuit on beautiful Belle Isle and was never headed. His Raybestos Mustang was .237 of a second ahead of the Sunoco Camaro piloted by Ron Fellows at the end. Tommy Kendall picked up fastest qualifier honors again, and a fourth place finish. His teammate Boris Said III started third, finished the same way. The fastest race lap was driven by Greg Pickett in the Cytomax/Rain-X Camaro, who rounded out the top five. Schroeder's front running victory was his third of the year. No other driver has won more than once. At the season's halfway mark Schroeder appears to be the man to beat for the '96 Trans-Am driver's title.

Trans-Am Championship Race 8
ATCALL Trans-Am Classic
Cleveland, Ohio
June 29, 1996
42 Laps, 99.54 Miles

TOMMY KENDALL TAKES CLEVELAND'S ATCALL CLASSIC

Tommy Kendall and teammate Boris Said III split the front running honors in Cleveland's ATCALL Classic. Said took the lead for the first third of the 42 lap event on the fast Burke Lakefront Airport circuit. Kendall neatly handled those duties for the final two thirds, after posting the fastest qualifying time. Despite running the fastest race laps, Said faded to ninth at the end. Kendall's closest pursuer was Greg Pickett in the Cytomax/Rain-X Camaro, racking up yet another fine second place, ahead of Mustang man Dorsey Schroeder and teammate Scott Sharp in the Rain-X Oil Energizer Camaro. The race was remarkably accident free, which led to a very rapid 113.40 mph average speed for the winner.

Trans-Am Championship Race 9
Children's Grand Prix of Minnesota
Minneapolis, Minnesota
July 7, 1996
63 Laps, 100.8 Miles

TOMMY KENDALL MAKES MINNEAPOLIS HIS THIRD WIN OF '96

This time Tommy Kendall let fellow Ford driver Dorsey Schroeder take fastest qualifying honors, while he, Kendall, made off with the Children's Grand Prix victory. Kendall allowed polesitter Paul Gentilozzi, in the HighwayMaster Camaro, to run up front for the first four laps, then took over the lead on lap five. Kendall ran out the next 59 laps enroute to victory circle. Perennial rival Ron Fellows did his best to dislodge Kendall from the lead, but had to settle for second place, .894 of a second astern of the flying Mustang man at the finish. Scott Sharp, in the Rain-X Oil Energizer, was a close third, ahead of Jamie Galles, in the ICI/Glidden Camaro, and early leader Gentilozzi, the fourth and fifth place finishers.

Trans-Am Championship Race 10
Grand Prix Player's de Trois-Rivieres
Trois-Rivieres, Quebec, Canada
August 4, 1996
55 Laps, 82.83 Miles

CANADIAN RON FELLOWS TAKES TROIS-RIVIERES

Back in his home country, Toronto's Ron Fellows was unbeatable in the Player's backed Trans-Am round at Trois-Rivieres. Polesitter Scott Sharp, in the Rain-X Oil Energizer Camaro led the first 15 laps. All the rest belonged to Fellows and his Sunoco Camaro. Dorsey Schroeder, in the Raybestos Mustang, edged Sharp for second place, with fourth going to Highway-Master Camaro driver, Paul Gentilozzi who started on the front row. Tommy Kendall, posted the fastest race lap, finished eighth after starting next to last due to qualifying problems, won the Optima Batteries Quick Charger Award.

Trans-Am Championship Race 11
Serengeti Eyewear Trans-Am Classic
Watkins Glen, New York
August 10, 1996
42 Laps, 102.9 Miles

SCHROEDER DOMINATES AT WATKINS GLEN

Dorsey Schroeder outsprinted polesitter Paul Gentilozzi into the first turn, was in charge of the Serengeti Eyewear Classic at Watkins Glen all the way. The only exception to Schroeder's dominance was an eight lap period when Boris Said III held sway. Repassed by Schroeder, Said held on for third place at the finish. Said's teammate, Tommy Kendall edged him for runner-up honors. Ron Fellows, winner of the previous round, figured to be tough opposition on this difficult circuit but lasted only four laps. Gentilozzi and Jamie Galles crashed after completing 33 laps. Said turned in the race's fastest lap.

Trans-Am Championship Race 12
Texaco-Havoline 200 Classic
Elkhart Lake, Wisconsin
August 16, 1996
25 Laps, 100 Miles

KENDALL & SAID TAKE ELKHART LAKE HONORS

Teammates Tommy Kendall, in the All Sport Mustang, and Boris Said III, in the Lion's Pride Mustang, led every lap of the Texaco-Havoline Classic at the Elkhart Lake circuit. Said was in front for the first half, Kendall the all important second half. Of the rest, Raybestos driver, Dorsey Schroeder came closest but he was no threat to the first two Mustang men. Once again Kendall was the fastest qualifier and proved his mettle by getting out front from his mandated fifth starting position. Jamie Galles, who started on the pole, was again a crash victim, while title contender Ron Fellows finished fifth, just behind Brian Simo.

Geoffrey Hewitt

Steve Mohlenkamp

Trans-Am Championship Race 13
Grand Prix of Dallas
Dallas, Texas
September 1, 1996
77 Laps, 100.1 Miles

Trans-Am Championship Race 14
Reno Grand Prix
Reno, Nevada
September 22, 1996
75 Laps, 95.25 Miles

FELLOWS DRIVES CAMARO TO DALLAS VICTORY

Ron Fellows, on the pole, was quickly ousted from the lead by Boris Said III who continued in command til the two thirds mark of the race. Not to be denied, Fellows regained the top spot on lap 57, setting the fastest race lap on the way, and cruised to victory by the comfortable margin of 11.059 seconds. Tommy Kendall, again the fastest qualifier, in the All Sport Body Quencher Mustang, pipped Said, in the Graingers Mustang, for runner-up honors. Dorsey Schroeder, the second fastest qualifier, saw his title hopes take a bad bounce when suspension failure set in after 53 laps of the 77 scheduled. Jon Gooding had a good day, in the Mountain Dew Mustang, finishing fourth.

RON FELLOWS ROLLS TO RENO VICTORY

It wasn't enough to gain him the Trans-Am driver's title, but Ron Fellows finished the '96 season in handsome style, adding victory in Reno's season closing race to his win in Dallas' penultimate round. Fellows did earn third place in the championship. Tommy Kendall was the fastest qualifier, finished fourth, cruised to his second Trans-Am Championship in a row. Jamie Galles chased Fellows home in the race, 2.082 seconds behind. Third place Tom Gloy, in a rare appearance as a driver, proved that he can still handle the assignment behind the wheel as well as field front running cars. Dorsey Schroeder again suffered mechanical disappointment, settled for second in the championship.

POST SEASON NOTES 1996 AWARDS

Max Lagod won the Raybestos Rising Star of the Year award on the basis of seven top ten finishes. He missed four rounds of the series and thereby missed out on Rookie of the Year honors which went to John Miller. Greg Pickett, one of the best liked competitors on the circuit and still one of the fastest, was honored for his contributions to the series with a special Trans-Am Milestone award. R.J. Valentine took a risky route to the year's Optima Batteries Quick Charger Award. He started dead last, moved up 15 places to the 11th finishing slot, and Optima honors for the race. For the year, he was 20 points ahead of second place Optima competitor Jon Gooding.

Ford notched the Manufacturers' Championship.

Geoffrey Hewitt

Dan Bianchi

Banner Year for Racer/Businessman R.J. Valentine

Long one of the top independents in a series dominated by factory teams, R.J. Valentine capped his 16 year Trans-Am career by winning the Optima Batteries Quick Charger Award. The award pays points for every place a driver improves his finishing position over his starting position. In the course of picking up the award, Valentine finished higher than his starting position everytime out save one, where he fell to transmission problems. He picked up four first ten finishes along the way. Perhaps his finest outing was in the season finale at Reno, where he moved up from 26th and last on the grid to an 11th place finish, just missing the top ten. At Homestead, Valentine joined the elite group of Trans-Am drivers who have made more than 100 starts in the series. Of the five, four are still active: Greg Pickett, Paul Gentilozzi, Jim Derhaag, and Valentine.

Andy Evans

Roberto Muller

Jack Long

Richard Bowen

IMSA Reborn

With IMSA on the block for most of the year, the on again, off again sale of the sanctioning organization overshadowed one of its most exciting competition years in a decade. All the speculation went out the window in September when international marketing executive Roberto Muller and IMSA jointly announced the sale of the group to Muller. Chief financial backer and key mover in the new corporate group IMSG was Andy Evans, a long term and highly competitive IMSA car owner and driver with an equally lengthy background as a financial executive. With Evans making the moves, the new group quickly injected the capital and management talent IMSA needed to regain its glory. At the operational level Jack Long, one time organizer of the Canadian Grand Prix and

Molson Indy Toronto was recruited from his current job as Tony George's right hand man in the newly formed Indy Racing League. As Executive Director of the new group, he brings a wealth of hands on management experience. The new group swiftly brought in outside talent for the other key operational posts. After a very brief period, of the old IMSA executives, only Ed Nicholls remains. He was promoted to Public Relations Director. As evidence of marketing know how, Virgin Atlantic Interactive signed on immediately as presenting sponsor. As evidence of capital commitment, the new group bought the Sebring and Mosport tracks, made it clear that further purchases were on the horizon. In view of Evans' background, it would appear that a public offering of a corporation consisting of

a sanctioning group, race tracks, and merchandising operations was in the offing.

Those following IMSA's fortunes were encouraged by the fact that entries for the '97 Rolex 24 at Daytona totalled over 100 and advance ticket sales for the event were the largest ever, both items that should please Richard Bowen of sponsor Exxon. Evans can bring experience from both sides of the pit wall to bear on his new project having been a front running competitor not only in the IMSA series, where he has posted several victories in his WSC Ferrari 333 SP, but the 24 Hours of LeMans as well. With co-driver Fermin Velez, the '95 IMSA WSC champion, he is a favorite for top honors in the 1997 Rolex 24 at Daytona, and the Exxon Superflo 12 Hours of Sebring.

Wayne Taylor and Oldsmobile Frustrate Ferrari, Take Exxon World Sportscar Championship

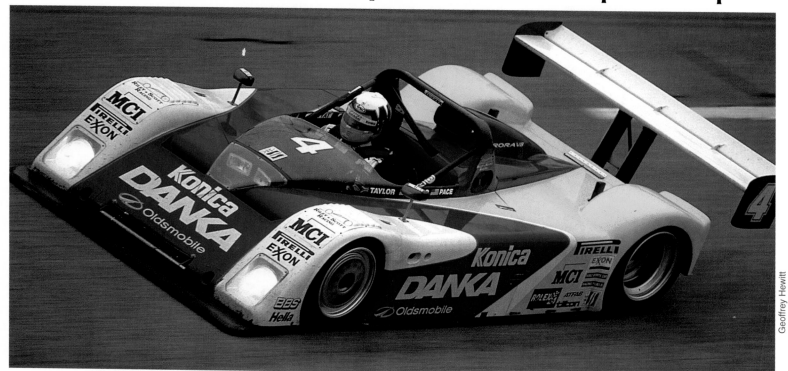

Geoffrey Hewitt

Wayne Taylor is short, mild-mannered, wears glasses, looks nothing like the popular conception of a world class racing driver. Put him behind the wheel of a World Sports Car, however, and he immediately assumes a different dimension. Perhaps he orders his driving suits from the same source that supplies Superman his capes. In the first year of the Exxon backed series for these unique two-seaters he won the championship in an unlikely vehicle, a Kudzu Mazda, against the best that more prominent manufacturers could throw at him. In '95, he switched to one of the all-conquering Ferrari 333 SPs, and, though he didn't retain his title, proved he could handle highly sophisticated 12 cylinder machinery as well as more mundane concoctions. In '96, he and faithful sponsors Danka and Konica switched to an all American package; Olds power and homebred Riley & Scott chassis. With help from co-drivers Eric Van de Poele and Jim Pace, he started out in striking fashion, winning both the Rolex 24 at Daytona and the Exxon Superflo 12 Hours of Sebring, the crown jewels in the IMSA sanctioned series. Not that Ferrari was taking its '95 Manufacturers' Championship lightly. Factory

test driver Max Papis was "made available" to Gianpiero Moretti's team. Papis responded with pole positions in both of the big races and brilliant driving stints but couldn't prevail in either. Andy Evans took former Formula One drivers Michele Alboreto and Mauro Baldi aboard his long distance race effort and they, too, fell short in the opening events. Rain-X backed Rob Dyson entered a pair of potent, well driven, Ford powered Riley & Scotts in the fray but they would come on strong only later in the season, winning the last three events with Butch Leitzinger and John Paul Jr. starring behind the wheel.

Papis and Ferrari were, of course, too potent to be denied all year. Road Atlanta fell to the dashing Italian and Moretti's red Ferrari speedster. In Texas, Taylor and Pace, plus Scott Sharp turned the tables. With IMSA returning to the traditional venues of Lime Rock and Watkins Glen, Papis put on crowd pleasing late race runs to prevail at both. With Sharp back again to assist, Taylor tamed Sears Point.

Now it was Ford's turn, as John Paul Jr. and Butch Leitzinger put the Rain-X backed Dyson car into victory circle at Mosport, Dallas, and Daytona's season ending three hour

event. Throughout the season, down to the Daytona finale, Taylor maintained his consistency. Papis, for all his speed and fire, was not so fortunate. His car was an early drop out at Dallas. For the final countdown, Taylor only had to start at Daytona to take the driving title for the second time. He did just that.

In IMSA's Exxon Supreme GT Championship, the only factory assisted teams in the big GTS-1 division were those powered by Oldsmobile. Predictably, an Olds Aurora driver, Irv Hoerr, won the title, with manufacturers' honors going to Olds. Eight of the ten events were won by Olds drivers, with Hoerr teammate Darin Brassfield, Brian Cunningham and the family team of Charles and Rob Morgan also getting into the win column. The only exceptions were Sebring which fell to the Porsche team of Hans Stuck and Bill Adams and the Daytona finale which went to Stu Hayner and Chevrolet. GTS-2 was more hotly contested with the manufacturers' title going to BMW and Porsche's Larry Schumacher taking the drivers' title. At GTS-2 Porsche with a "United Nations" driving team was a star performer at Daytona placing a lofty fourth overall and first in class.

Rolex Watch USA President Roland Puton distributes the winners' spoils to Wayne Taylor, Jim Pace and Scott Sharp after their victory, the closest ever, in the Rolex 24 at Daytona. The trio drove an Olds R&S MKIII, the first all American car to win.

One minute short after 24 hours: "Mad Max" Papis and the Momo Ferrari 333 SP almost caught Wayne Taylor's winning Danka Olds in a stirring late race chase.

Geoffrey Hewitt

Exxon World Sportscar/Exxon
Supreme GT Championship Race 1
Rolex 24 at Daytona
Daytona International Speedway
Daytona Beach, Florida
February 3-4, 1996
3.56 Mile Road/Oval Course

ROLEX 24 AT DAYTONA GOES TO OLDS TRIO OF TAYLOR, SHARP & PACE

FERRARI CHALLENGE MISSES BY ONE MINUTE

While Rolex Watch USA President Roland Puton was handing the winners' spoils to Olds-powered Wayne Taylor, Scott Sharp and Jim Pace, their race-long antagonists the Ferrari 333 SP mounted team of Gianpiero Moretti, Bob Wollek, Didier Theys and Max Papis were bemoaning their bad luck. A

minor mishap took them from likely winners to downcast runners-up. The tiny gremlin was a loose gearbox bolt, which forced the leading Ferrari to make an unscheduled pit stop around 9:00 AM when it enjoyed a three lap cushion over the then second place Olds. The Olds, too, had gearbox problems, but they were surmountable. Fifteen minutes later the Ferrari emerged, now down four laps. "Mad Max" Papis led the charge to get back on top, and a thrilling charge it was. Unfortunately Papis' heroics fell just over a minute short, the closest finish in the event's 34 year history. The Olds victory in a Riley & Scott chassis was the first ever for an all American car. Once the race settled down, the top two finishers engaged in a seesaw battle, exchanging the lead 14 times. Third overall went to Kudzu proponent Jim Downing, aided by Butch Hamlet, Tim McAdam and Barry Waddell. Almost unbelievable was the fourth

place overall, first in GTS-2 placement of a Porsche 911 Carrera RSR driven by Lilian Bryner, Enzo Calderari, Ulrich Richter and Ferdinand de Lesseps. Bryner was the only female in the race and the quartet repeated their class win of 1995.

GTS-1 honors went to Olds Aurora, with Rob and Charles Morgan, Joe Pezza and Jon Gooding sharing driving duties. They placed seventh overall. Fifth overall was another Olds WSC car with Franck Freon, Lee Payne and Ross Bentley the drivers. Second in GTS-2 and also ahead of all the GTS-1 entries was the Porsche 911 of Cort Wagner, Steve Dente, Mike Doolin and Richard Raimist. 76 cars took the starter's flag and there were some breathtaking accidents including that of Bill Adam in a Porsche, Kenny Acheson in the Lister Storm, and Irv Hoerr in an Aurora. No serious injuries were reported.

Exxon World Sportscar/Exxon
Supreme GT Championship Race 2
Exxon Superflo 12 Hours of Sebring
Presented by Aurora
Sebring International Raceway
Sebring, Florida
March 16, 1996
3.6 Mile Road Course

WAYNE TAYLOR AND OLDSMOBILE TAKE TOP HONORS AT SEBRING

Wayne Taylor and company (Eric Van de Poele and Jim Pace) wasted no time in proving that their Olds powered victory at Daytona was no fluke. This time they were a full four laps ahead of the best placed Ferrari, the 333 SP of Michele Alboreto, Mauro Baldi and Andy Evans at the end of 12 hours on the historic Sebring circuit. The Daytona runners-up, Max Papis, Didier Theys and Gianpiero Moretti again started on the pole, placed third, nine laps down to Taylor's Danka/Konica Olds R&S MKIII. Admittedly both Ferraris had problems. One tangled with a slower car, the second tangled with major debris on the course. Taylor and company motored without incident. The Rain-X Ford R&S MKIII had two sojourns up front with Butch Letizinger and Andy Wallace at the helm, finished just behind the fourth place Mazda Kudzu of Butch Hamlet, Barry Waddell and Jim Downing. Porsche protagonists Hans Stuck and Bill Adam beat out the fastest qualifying GTS-1 Oldsmobile of Irv Hoerr, Darin Brassfield and Brian Cunningham for top honors in the category. Porsche also nailed down the top placement in GTS-2 with the 911 chauffeured by Andy Pilgrim, William Pace and Larry Schumacher. A pair of interesting Dodge Vipers made a welcome addition to the competitor ranks, with the best placed checking in at 12th overall, sixth in GTS-1 in the hands of Joe Varde, George Robinson, Victor Sifton and Price Cobb.

After approximately three hours, the race for WSC and overall honors became a triangulated affair, with the two top Ferraris and Taylor's Olds swapping the lead regularly but Taylor's car cruised at the end to its four lap cushion over Maranello's best. 58 cars took the starter's flag. With the season's two longest events behind them, Taylor, Pace, along with Oldsmobile, were firmly in front in the championship chase.

Geoffrey Hewitt

Steve Mohlenkamp

Exxon World Sportscar/Exxon
Supreme GT Championship Race 3
Grand Prix of Atlanta
Presented by Advance Auto Parts
Road Atlanta
Braselton, Georgia
April 21, 1996
2.52 Mile Road Course

FERRARI'S MAX PAPIS PREVAILS IN ATLANTA THREE HOUR

Max Papis put the Momo Ferrari 333 SP on the pole again at Atlanta. This time he put it in victory circle as well, even overcoming the time deficit he inherited from co-driver Gianpiero Moretti. Along the way, he set the fastest race lap. Wayne Taylor, going it alone in the Olds R&S MKIII finished two laps in arrears in second place. He was nursing a replacement engine after blowing his primary motor in practice. Ross Bentley got his first IMSA WSC podium finish in another Olds R&S MKIII, ahead of a second Momo entered Ferrari, this one driven by Gerry Jackson and Didier Theys. A perennial favorite of IMSA fans, James Weaver, along with Butch Leitzinger in the Rain-X Ford R&S

MKIII had second place well in hand when sidelined by mechanical problems. Don Clark and Craig T. Nelson brought another Ford powered R&S MKIII home fifth. With the top Porsche entries who contested GTS-1 at Daytona and Sebring missing, Olds drivers Darin Brassfield and Irv Hoerr readily picked up the honors in this category. Brian Cunningham in a similar car was just behind them.

In the separate (and shorter) GTS-2 event, Henry Taleb, in a well raced Nissan 240SX, humbled the factory assisted BMWs. Pete Halsmer finished second in his M3 followed by Jeff Purner's Porsche.

Exxon World Sportscar/Exxon
Supreme GT Championship Race 4
Exxon Superflo 500
Texas World Speedway
College Station, Texas
May 5, 1996
1.92 Mile Oval/Road Course

WAYNE TAYLOR AND OLDS TOP THE FERRARIS AT TEXAS WORLD SPEEDWAY

This time Wayne Taylor and his Olds R&S MKIII out-qualified the Ferrari 333 SPs. With some help from Jim Pace he out-finished them as well, just as he had at Daytona and Sebring. It was not a banner day for the Momo 333 SP Ferraris. The Didier Theys-Gerry Jackson pair fared best, checking in at fourth overall. The Max Papis-Gianpiero Moretti duo languished even further down in seventh place. The Ross Bentley-Anthony Lazzaro Olds finished second, on the same lap as the winners, 29.308 seconds in arrears. James Weaver and Andy Wallace dominated the race's midsection, keeping their Rain-X Ford R&S MKIII out in front for 136 of the 261 laps contested before slipping to third place at the finish. Taylor increased his points lead and served notice that he was the man to beat for the 1996 drivers' championship.

The top GTS-1 finisher, the Olds Aurora of Irv Hoerr and Darin Brassfield beat most of the WSC cars with its fifth place overall finish. In the GTS-2 bracket Porsches predominated. Andy Pilgrim and Larry Schumacher topped the category, followed by the 911s of Jeff Purner-Charles Cohen and Cort Wagner-Brent Martini-Kelly Collins. Boris Said, the fastest GTS-1 qualifier, in a Ford Mustang, lost his strong bid, falling to a failed waterpump. 26 starters took the green flag and there were no accidents of any consequence.

Geoffrey Hewitt

Geoffrey Hewitt

Exxon World Sportscar/Exxon
Supreme GT Championship Race 5
ATCALL Presents the
Dodge Dealers Grand Prix
at Lime Rock
Lime Rock Park
Lakeville, Connecticut
May 27, 1996
1.54 Mile Road Course

MAX PAPIS & FERRARI EDGE JAMES WEAVER & FORD AT LIME ROCK

James Weaver is one tough driver to pass, particularly when he has won the pole in the Rain-X Ford R&S MKIII, and led for 50 laps with only two to go. Max Papis, however, was up to this daunting task, got around Weaver, and booted his Ferrari 333 SP home with .571 of a second to spare. Butch Leitzinger, in the second Rain-X car, finished third, while Wayne Taylor, still the series points leader, finished fourth. Only the top quartet completed the 98 laps scheduled. Down a lap in fifth place was the second 333 SP, handled by Didier Theys and Fredy Lienhard.

Olds Aurora mounted Irv Hoerr had an easy time in capturing GTS-1 honors by more than seven laps over Dan Osterholt in an Olds Cutlass. Hoerr's teammate, Darin Brassfield wasn't as fortunate. He lasted only 14 laps. In the separate GTS-2 event Henry Taleb again brought his Nissan 240SX home ahead of the BMW contingent, led by Pete Halsmer and Bill Auberlen in M3s. Taleb led all of the 62 laps except the first two.

Exxon World Sportscar/Exxon
Supreme GT Championship Race 6
First Union Six Hours of the Glen
Presented by Acxiom
Watkins Glen International
Watkins Glen, New York
June 9, 1996
3.4 Mile Road Course

MAX PAPIS SUPERB IN SIX HOURS OF THE GLEN

Max Papis was again the fastest qualifier - and the fastest finisher - in winning the First Union Six Hours of the Glen in the Momo Ferrari 333 SP. His primary victim, the loser in a thrilling late race duel, was Butch Leitzinger, the redoubtable Ford R&S MKIII exponent. Not even a couple of off course excursions of his own making and another the result of a shunt with Wayne Taylor could stop the flying Papis. Gianpiero Morettii shared the driving duties in the 333 SP, but it was Papis who kept it out front and flying. Third place went to Wayne Taylor and Jim Pace in their

Olds R&S MKIII while a second Ford R&S MKIII piloted by John Paul Jr., Rob Dyson and James Weaver finished fourth, three laps down on the top three. Irv Hoerr again was top man in GTS-1, assisted by Darin Brassfield, Brian Cunningham and Brian DeVries. Porsche protagonist Hurley Haywood, with help from Tom Hessert, was the top performer in GTS-2 posting a handsome eighth overall. Papis was clearly the driver of the day and the darling of the crowd. He also caught up to Wayne Taylor in the championship chase. Both now stood at 164 points.

Geoffrey Hewitt

Geoffrey Hewitt

Exxon World Sportscar/Exxon
Supreme GT Championship Race 7
Toshiba California Grand Prix
Sears Point Raceway
Sonoma, California
July 14, 1996
2.52 Mile Road Course

WAYNE TAYLOR STAVES OFF FERRARI CHALLENGE AT SEARS POINT

Only .198 of a second separated Olds exponent Wayne Taylor and fast closing Ferrari driver Max Papis after three hours on the challenging Sears Point circuit. Butch Leitzinger took the pole, and, with John Paul Jr., led every lap but four in the Rain-X Ford R&S MKIII. With only two circuits remaining, fuel shortage put paid to his quest for a first victory of '96. Not only did Taylor get by without a contest, so did Papis. John Paul was able to salvage third, small consolation for a sterling effort gone astray. Taylor's win had Hollywood overtures. He spun out in practice, got banged solidly by another competitor and was carted off to the hospital. Since he had, previously in his career, broken his neck, and now had pain in the same region, he thought his season and his bid for a second championship might be over. Not so. Taylor's car was repaired and xrays showed him fit to take the wheel. The courageous South African then gave the Olds an inspired ride to win the race and recapture the undisputed lead in the championship tussle.

Irv Hoerr and Darin Brassfield were again the winners in GTS-1. In the separate GTS-2 event, BMW's efforts paid off, with Pete Halsmer, the polesitter, and Bill Auberlen finishing 1-2 in M3s.

Exxon World Sportscar/Exxon
Supreme GT Championship Race 8
Chrysler Mosport 500
Mosport Park
Bowmanville, Ontario, Canada
August 25, 1996
2.459 Mile Road Course

JOHN PAUL JR, BUTCH LEITZINGER, & FORD FLY AT MOSPORT, EDGE FERRARI TEAM

So close, so often, John Paul Jr. and Butch Leitzinger could not be denied victory at Mosport. Their Rain-X Ford R&S MKIII flashed into victory circle a mere .189 of a second ahead of the Didier Theys-Max Papis Ferrari 333 SP, which was followed across the finish line by the second Momo 333 SP which listed Gianpiero Moretti as well as Theys in the driving lineup. Although Papis put his car on the pole, he was out-accelerated into the first corner and the Ford powered car led for 17 laps. Except for three laps that went to Fermin Velez, the '96 WSC Champion, in a 333 SP, and a single lap which went to Wayne Taylor in the Olds powered R&S MKIII and one to the second 333 SP, the rest of the race belonged to the two top finishers who swapped the lead five times in the course of the three hours. Taylor ended up fourth, clung to a precarious one point lead over Papis in the title chase. Velez, sharing driving duties with Antonio Hermann, notched fifth place.

GTS-1 went to Irv Hoerr in an Olds Aurora in another winning performance, after qualifying first in the category. Boris Said III was the quickest GTS-2 qualifier in a BMW M3. With help from Pete Halsmer he translated his qualifying honors into a class win and made the top ten overall. BMW was now on a roll in the GTS-2 manufacturers chase.

Shelly Schmidt

Geoffrey Hewitt

Exxon World Sportscar/Exxon Supreme GT Championship Race 9
Sprint Grand Prix of Dallas
Presented by Exxon Superflo
Dallas Street Circuit
Dallas, Texas
September 1, 1996
1.5 Mile Temporary Street Circuit

BUTCH LEITZINGER AND FORD MAKE IT TWO IN A ROW AT DALLAS

Going solo this time, Butch Leitzinger brought his Rain-X Ford MKIII home in front in Dallas' two hour street circuit event. It was a great weekend for the Rob Dyson entered Fords. His second car, driven by James Weaver and John Paul Jr., took third place. Wayne Taylor, locked in a season long battle for the title with Max Papis, had a relatively easy day at the office, picked up second place. Papis had incredibly bad luck. He severely damaged his primary 333 SP in practice and watched in disbelief as the second Momo 333 SP which he was slated to co-drive limped into the pits with a broken suspension after only three laps. With only one race remaining, the swift Italian had a mathematical chance, but, realistically, no chance at all of catching Taylor. Eliseo Salazar put his Ferrari 333 SP on the pole and looked to be a winner until he cut a tire late in the race. Hustling to make up time, he tangled with a GTS-1 driver and tagged the wall. Salazar had already compiled enough laps to finish fourth.

In GTS-1 a familiar face was draped in the winner's laurels, Irv Hoerr, yet again, the fastest qualifier. Hoerr clinched the drivers' title for himself and the Manufacturers' Championship for Oldsmobile. In the separate GTS-2 event Pete Halsmer, BMW M3 mounted, beat a pair of Porsches handled by Larry Schumacher and Cort Wagner and fellow BMW pilot Boris Said III to the checker.

Exxon World Sportscar/Exxon
Supreme GT Championship Race 10
Daytona IMSA Finale
Daytona International Speedway
Daytona Beach, Florida
October 6, 1996
3.56 Mile Road/Oval Course

DAYTONA FINALE GOES TO FORD'S BUTCH LEITZINGER AND JOHN PAUL JR.

Butch Leitzinger and John Paul Jr. made it a sweep of the season's last three races in their Rain-X Ford Riley & Scott MKIII. Starting on the pole, they led the first 17 laps, the last seven, and 51 in between, while piling up a huge 29.346 second cushion at the end. Not that the Ferraris didn't try. Didier Theys nosed his 333 SP in front twice, gained the runner-up honors. Wayne Taylor, who opted not to put his imminent championship at risk with an all-out effort, cruised to the third finishing spot and the title with co-driver Jim Pace. Max Papis' last ditch shot at the 1996 drivers' title predictably fell short. He finished fourth, aided by Gianpiero Moretti in today's race. Papis, however, salvaged the runner-up slot in the championship. Wayne Taylor's two championships in three years is a pretty respectable average in any league.

The first GTS-1 finisher, was for the second time in '96, not an Olds.

Stu Hayner and Roger Schramm brought their Chevrolet Corvette home eighth overall, first in GTS-1. Irv Hoerr, already the GTS-1 title-holder, finished second after another fastest qualifier effort. GTS-2 went to a BMW again, this one driven by Javier Quiros. Oldsmobile had already taken the manufacturers' title in GTS-1. GTS-2 manufacturers' honors went to BMW although Porsche pilot Larry Schumacher earned the drivers' honors in the division.

Interestingly, the Olds-Ferrari battle for manufacturers' honors in the premier WSC category had to be decided on a tie breaker after each scored 227 points, with Ford a close third at 213. The nod went to Olds on the basis of four victories to three for Ferrari, an indication of how close the WSC competition was in '96.

Shelly Schmidt

Geoffrey Hewitt

1 Ferrari Nemesis... **Wayne Taylor** won IMSA's big two, Daytona and Sebring, fended off Ferraris for his second Exxon World Sportscar Championship in three years. (260 WSC points)

2 Rapid Rookie... **Max Papis** displayed speed and virtuosity but one "bad luck" weekend relegated him and Ferrari to second place. (245 WSC points)

Shelly Schmidt

3 Three in a Row... **Butch Leitzinger** swept the last three races of the year, served notice that he and Ford will be hard to beat in '97. (240 WSC points)

4 Ferrari Exponent... **Didier Theys**, a front runner all year, fell just short of the winner's circle. (224 WSC points)

Shelly Schmidt

5 Solid Progress... **Ross Bentley** made a big upward movement in '96. (167 WSC points)

6 Fast Ford Man... **John Paul Jr.** co-drove with Leitzinger in two of Ford's three wins. (158 WSC points)

7 Fan Favorite... **James Weaver** lost none of his spectacular driving skills but couldn't match '95 results. (153 WSC points)

8 Owner/Driver... **Gianpiero Moretti** entered and co-drove Papis' Ferrari, equaled him in spirit if not in speed. (151 WSC points)

9 Taylor Teammate... **Jim Pace** co-drove in three of Wayne Taylor's four victories. (139 WSC points)

Geoffrey Hewitt

Shelly Schmidt

10 First Time First Tenner... **Barry Waddell** joined the elite company of WSC's ten best. (135 WSC points)

1996 IMSA WSC Drivers' Championship Points

Position	Driver	Chassis/Engine	Points
1	WAYNE TAYLOR	R&S Mark III Oldsmobile	260
2	MASSIMILIANO "MAX" PAPIS	Ferrari 333 SP Ferrari	245
3	BUTCH LEITZINGER	R&S Mark III Ford	240
4	DIDIER THEYS	Ferrari 333 SP Ferrari	224
5	ROSS BENTLEY	R&S Mark III Oldsmobile	167
6	JOHN PAUL JR.	R&S Mark III Ford	158
7	JAMES WEAVER	R&S Mark III Ford	153
8	GIANPIERO MORETTI	Ferrari 333 SP Ferrari	151
9	JIM PACE	R&S Mark III Oldsmobile	139
10	BARRY WADDELL	Kudzu Mazda	135
11	JIM DOWNING	Kudzu Mazda	82
12	SCOTT SCHUBOT	Courage C41 Chevrolet	78
13	ANDY WALLACE	R&S Mark III Ford	75
14	HENRY CAMFERDAM	Hawk Chevrolet	75
15	JEFF JONES	Argo JM-20 Chevrolet	66
16	CRAIG T. NELSON	R&S Mark III Ford	62
17	SCOTT SHARP	R&S Mark III Oldsmobile	60
18	ROGER MANDEVILLE	Hawk Chevrolet	60
19	TOM VOLK	Kudzu Chevrolet	58
20	BLAKE PRIDGEN	Argo JM-20 Chevrolet	54
21	JAY COCHRAN	R&S Mark III Oldsmobile	51
22	BUTCH HAMLET	Kudzu Mazda	50
23	DAN CLARK	R&S Mark III Ford	43
24	BRUCE TRENNERY	Cannibal Chevrolet	38
	GRAHAME BRYANT	Cannibal Chevrolet	38
	JEFFERY PATTINSON	Cannibal Chevrolet	38
27	JOHN JONES	Argo JM-20 Chevrolet	37
28	ELISEO SALAZAR	Ferrari 333 SP Ferrari	34
29	ERIC VAN DE POELE	Ferrari 333 SP Ferrari	33
30	FREDY LIENHARD	Ferrari 333 SP Ferrari	33
31	NEIL JAMISON	Magnum Buick	33
32	JOHN MIRRO	Kudzu Buick	31
33	MAURO BALDI	Ferrari 333 SP Ferrari	29
34	FRANCK FREON	R&S Mark III Oldsmobile	26
	LEE PAYNE	R&S Mark III Oldsmobile	26

1996 IMSA WSC Manufacturers' Points

Position	Manufacturer	Points
1	OLDSMOBILE	227
2	FERRARI	227
3	FORD	213
4	CHEVROLET	113
5	BUICK	81
6	MAZDA	75
7	BMW	49
8	CADILLAC	14
9	PONTIAC	7

Andy Evans' red Scandia Ferrari 333 SP with '95 WSC Champion Fermin Velez co-driving.

Rob Dyson's Rain-X Ford R&S MKIII with Butch Leitzinger, winner of the final three '96 events, co-driving.

Shelly Schmidt

1 Repeat Champion... **Irv Hoerr** was again the king in Olds - dominated GTS-1. (218 GTS-1 points)

Shelly Schmidt

1 Porsche Protagonist... **Larry Schumacher** beat out a swarm of BMW drivers for individual honors in GTS-2. (200 GTS-2 points)

2 Hoerr's Teammate... **Darin Brassfield** was the other half of the Olds mounted driver team that swept GTS-1 honors. (187 GTS-1 points)

Shelly Schmidt

2 BMW's Best... **Pete Halsmer** gained runner-up honors in GTS-2, was instrumental in BMW's manufacturers' title. (185 GTS-2 points)

Shelly Schmidt